PointMaker™ Object Lessons for Youth Ministry

Group
LOVELAND, COLORADO

PointMaker™ Object Lessons for Youth Ministry

Visit our Web site: **www.grouppublishing.com**

Credits
Contributing Authors: Katrina Arbuckle, Karen Dockrey, Stacy L. Haverstock, Michelle Ransom Hicks, Jan Kershner, Pamela Malloy, Kelly Martin, Erin McKay, Julie Meiklejohn, Janet Dodge Narum, Todd Outcalt, Kristi Rector, Christina Schofield, Alison Simpson, Tim Simpson, Helen Turnbull, and Jane Vogel
Book Acquisitions Editor: Amy Simpson
Editor: Debbie Gowensmith
Creative Development Editor: Jim Kochenburger
Chief Creative Officer: Joani Schultz
Copy Editor: Dena Twinem
Art Director: Kari K. Monson
Computer Graphic Artist: Nighthawk Design and Tracy K. Donaldson
Cover Art Director: Jeff A. Storm
Cover Designer: Rick Dembicki
Cover Photographer: Tony Stone Images
Illustrator: Amy Bryant
Production Manager: Alexander Jorgensen

Library of Congress Cataloging-in-Publication Data
PointMaker object lessons for youth ministry / [contributing authors, Katrina Arbuckle … et al.].
p. cm.
Includes indexes.
ISBN 0-7644-2196-4 (alk. paper)
1. Church work with youth. I. Arbuckle, Katrina. II. Group Publishing.

BV4447 .P557 2000
268′.433--dc21 99-058642

10 9 8 7 6 5 4 09 08 07 06 05 04 03 02 01

Printed in the United States of America.

Contents

Indexes

Introduction

When we try to teach scriptural truths to our teenagers, are we giving them something they can relate to and understand? And are we teaching them in such a way that they'll *personally* grasp the truths they're introduced to?

It's essential that we help teenagers move from abstract thoughts of the Christian faith to concrete, real examples that help them see and hear and feel and smell and taste what it means to be a Christian.

PointMaker™ Object Lessons for Youth Ministry can help you do just that.

Object lessons help abstract thoughts take shape in the physical world. Suddenly, through building walls with rocks, sheets, or paper, students understand that they can trust God's rock-like strength and protection. Through trying to play a game without knowing the rules, students understand how God's Word can direct them.

For youth to really understand what object lessons are teaching, though, they must experience the object lesson themselves. With *PointMaker Object Lessons for Youth Ministry*, your teenagers do not simply sit and listen to you talk. They're involved. They participate. They experience firsthand the truth being taught. They become part of the object lesson themselves so the spiritual truth can take shape and meaning for each person.

So whenever you want your teenagers to experience a spiritual concept in a concrete way, reach for these object lessons. Use them as discussion starters; foundations for Bible studies; or strong, stand-alone pointmakers. The indexes will help you choose an object lesson with the Scripture or the theme you want to focus on.

Also utilize the extension ideas provided with some object lessons to take the learning a step further. And watch for the "outrageous idea" icon. Surprise your students with these out-of-the-ordinary lessons that teach with items like Spam, mousetraps, or pets.

Teaching teenagers to grow in Christian faith can be a tough job. There are a lot of complicated concepts to teach—concepts that, for a lot of teenagers, seem to float above their heads. Use *PointMaker Object Lessons for Youth Ministry* to help students rein in those concepts and more clearly understand their faith.

Object Lessons

Acting as the Hands of Christ

Theme: Servanthood
Scripture: Philippians 2:1-7
Supplies: You'll need a Bible and pens.

Use this discussion to consider how Christ was a servant and how we can be like Christ.

Have youth spend a few minutes studying their hands while they think of all the things their hands have done during the past week. Ask for volunteers to share some of the things their hands have done. Then ask:

- **What are some ways people can use their hands to help others?**
- **What are some ways people use their hands to hurt others?**

Ask a volunteer to read aloud Philippians 2:1-7. Ask:

- **In what ways was Christ a servant?**
- **How might we affect others if we serve others the way Christ did?**
- **How can we become more like Christ?**

Say: **Christ so often used his hands for acts of service. The ultimate act of service was when his hands were nailed to a cross for our sins.**

Ask:

- **How might we focus on making our hands servant's hands this week?**

Ask youth to commit to at least one act of service to perform during the coming week. Distribute pens, and have students write on their hands a word or symbol to signify their commitment.

And You Tell Two Friends

Theme: Sharing faith
Scripture: Acts 1:8
Supplies: You'll need index cards, pens, and Bibles.

Use this lesson to help students understand each of them has a role to play in sharing faith in Jesus Christ with others.

Ask for a student volunteer. Hand the volunteer a stack of index cards and a pen. Instruct the volunteer to look up Acts 1:8, write the verse on an index card, and give the card to another student. Tell the volunteer that he or she is to repeat the exercise, giving an index card to as many students as possible in two minutes.

After two minutes, count how many people have cards. Congratulate the volunteer on his or her efforts. Then ask:

- **What was difficult about our volunteer's assignment?**
- **What might have made our volunteer's job easier?**

Say: **It's difficult to try to reach everyone all by yourself. Let's discover another way to reach people.**

Explain that the same volunteer will write the verse on index cards again, but this time each person who receives an index card will also write verses on index cards to give to others. Distribute cards and pens. Have the volunteer begin; then call time after two minutes. Count how many people have cards, and congratulate the group for its efforts. Then have the students continue the exercise until everyone has an index card. Afterward, ask someone to read aloud an index card. Then ask:

- **What made the difference between our first effort and our second effort?**
- **What does that tell you about how to fulfill Acts 1:8?**

Say: **Jesus said, "You will be my witnesses in Jerusalem, and in all Judea and Samaria, and to the ends of the earth." "You" means all of us! And as you saw today, if we all tell others about Jesus, we can more easily and quickly reach more people.**

Have teenagers each write on their index cards the name of one person with whom they can share their faith. Encourage students to take home their cards as reminders to follow through.

Armed for Battle

Theme: God's Word

Scripture: Psalm 1:1-3; Matthew 4:1-11; Ephesians 6:11-17

Supplies: You'll need Bibles and scrap paper of two different colors (try the recycling bin).

Use this lesson to help students understand how disadvantaged they are when facing wickedness and evil without knowing the Word of God.

Have students form two teams, and explain that they're going to have a contest to see which team can throw the most paper wads at the other team. Designate an area of the room for each team to stand in, and indicate a line over which neither team can cross. Then give one team a large stack of one color of paper, and give the other team a very, very small stack of a different color of paper. The team with the small stack can only toss their color paper back to the other side. They cannot toss the other team's color of paper back at them. When students complain, ask them to play the game and see what happens.

Have teams begin, and call time after a couple of minutes. The greater number of paper wads should obviously be in the disadvantaged team's area.

Leave the paper wads where they lay, and instruct students to sit down in a circle. Have a volunteer read aloud Ephesians 6:11-17, and then ask:

- **What was it like to play this game without enough paper?**
- **How would fighting without armor be like playing without paper?**

Say: **God has given us the Bible to help us "stand against the devil's schemes." When we don't read or know the Bible, we leave ourselves exposed, unprotected; we're without a weapon. The battle becomes as one-sided as the game we played a few moments ago.**

Ask a volunteer to read aloud Matthew 4:1-11. Then ask:

- **How did Satan try to tempt Jesus?**
- **How did Jesus respond to Satan?**
- **How was trying to win the game we played without paper like trying to face Satan's temptation without knowing God's Word?**
- **Has recalling a Bible story or verse ever helped you to do the right thing? Explain.**

Distribute Bibles, and have students read aloud Psalm 1:1-3 together. Then have youth form groups of two to three and spend a few minutes memorizing a few of the verses they studied during this lesson.

Before students leave, have them gather up the paper wads and put them back in the recycling bin.

Extension Idea

Try this idea during the Bible memorization element of this object lesson. Have teenagers take turns tossing paper wads into a trash can. When they make a shot, they get to recite a Bible verse.

Avoid the Trap

Theme: Temptation

Scripture: 1 Corinthians 10:13; Ephesians 6:10-18

Supplies: You'll need scrap paper, pens, a mousetrap for each person, and a straw.

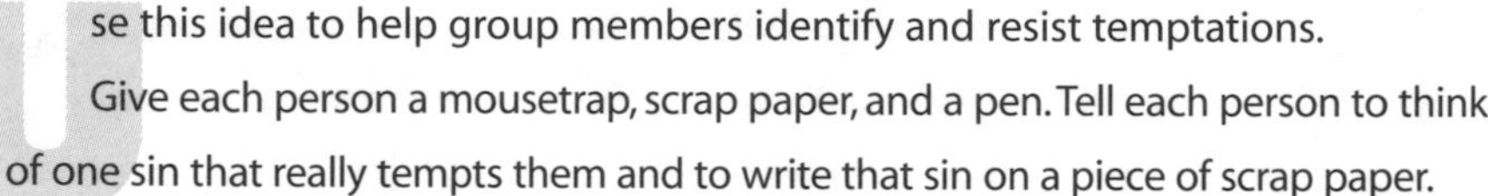

Use this idea to help group members identify and resist temptations.

Give each person a mousetrap, scrap paper, and a pen. Tell each person to think of one sin that really tempts them and to write that sin on a piece of scrap paper.

Then have group members make paper wads of their scrap-paper sins. Demonstrate how to place the paper wads in the mousetraps like bait. Gather group members in a circle, and have them sit with their mousetraps in front of them. Ask:

- **Where does temptation come from?**
- **How is temptation like a trap?**
- **What happens when you give in to temptation?**

Choose a mousetrap to set off, and be sure students are sitting at least a couple of feet from it. Then use a straw to trigger that mousetrap. Say: **Temptation is like a trap set by Satan. It's got to be a trap, or we'd never give in to temptation, would we? If each time we were tempted, Satan said, "Attention, please! This is Satan, and I'm about to try to make you sin," we would likely be able to resist. But that's not the way it works.**

Satan tries to make us think that the temptations are our own ideas and that there's nothing very wrong with what he's suggesting. And if we've given in to temptation before, Satan reminds us of that and accuses us of not really being Christians. Ask:

- **How do you usually try to resist temptation?**

Ask volunteers to read aloud 1 Corinthians 10:13 and Ephesians 6:10-18. Say: **The Bible tells us how to resist temptation. We should stay focused on God, read the Bible, and pray. Take your mousetraps home to remind you that temptation is a trap that God will help you resist.** Have students be sure their mousetraps are fixed so they won't accidentally be set off. Also have students leave their mousetraps in the room until they go home.

Balloon Burst

Theme: Envy
Scripture: Proverbs 14:30
Supplies: You'll need a Bible, a pitcher filled with water, a funnel, a small balloon, and towels.

Use this lesson to creatively explore the harm that envy causes.

Do this object lesson outside, if possible. If you do the lesson inside, you'll need a plastic basin or bucket to catch the water.

Have students sit in a circle. Place the balloon, the funnel, and the pitcher of water in the middle of the circle. Place the funnel in the neck of the balloon.

Explain that the group is going to fill up the balloon to represent things they want that others have—money, cars, or clothes, for example. Begin by naming something you often desire. As you do, pour some water into the balloon. Then have students take turns naming things they desire while pouring water into the balloon.

Continue around the circle until the balloon bursts. If everyone has had two turns and the balloon still hasn't burst, have a volunteer try to pick up the balloon. The extra pressure should cause the balloon to break.

After the balloon has burst, have students remain seated in the circle. Ask:

• Why do we want what others have?

• How was this activity like what happens when we focus on getting what others have?

Ask a volunteer to read aloud Proverbs 14:30. Ask:

• How does this Bible passage apply to the exercise we just did?

Say: **If we fill our hearts with envy, our lives will be rotten. But if we can be thankful for what we have and happy for others in what they have, our hearts will be full of peace.**

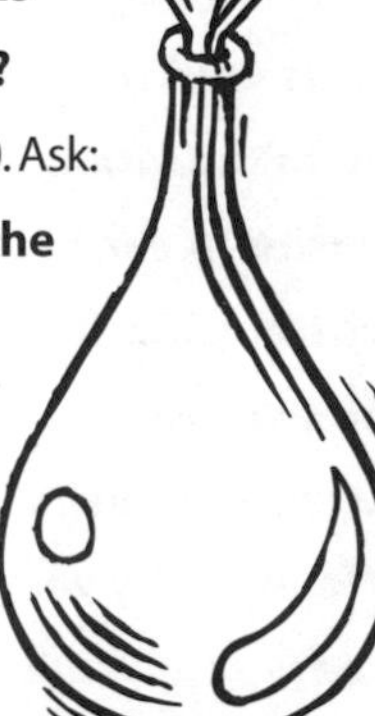

Be Holy

Theme: Holiness

Scripture: 1 Peter 1:14-16

Supplies: You'll need a Bible, a piece of fruit for each student, baby carrots, a cutting board, and a knife. Be sure to wash the fruit and carrots before the activity.

Use this lesson to show students the importance of being holy inside and out.

Distribute the pieces of fruit to teenagers. As they eat the fruit, have them discuss these questions:

• **How does the color of the outside of the fruit compare to the inside?**

• **How does the taste of the outside of the fruit compare to the inside?**

• **What's a person like who's different on the outside from on the inside as these pieces of fruit are?**

Ask a volunteer to read aloud 1 Peter 1:14-16.

Say: **Holiness can be difficult to understand. But all Christians are to live holy lives—lives that reflect God's holiness. How do we do that? How do we live holy lives?**

Have students gather around you, and cut a section of carrot for each student. Ask:

• **How does the color of the outside of the carrot compare to the inside?**

• **How does the taste of the outside of the carrot compare to the inside?**

• **What's a person like who's the same on the outside and the inside as these carrots are?**

Say: **God wants us to be like a carrot. A carrot is the same color and taste from the outside to the inside. What you see on the outside is exactly what you get on the inside. A carrot is consistent. God wants us to be the same on the inside and the outside. Instead of showing the world an act of holiness while continuing to conform to evil desires on the inside, we can strive to be holy on the outside and the inside as God is holy.**

As students finish eating the carrots and fruit, ask them to name ways that they can be more consistent and holy in all areas of their lives.

Beneath the Skin

Theme: False prophets
Scripture: Matthew 7:15-18
Supplies: You'll need Bibles and four masks that, if possible, reflect different personalities—mean, brave, sweet, and scary, for example.

Use this lesson to help students recognize the masks some people wear to hide their true selves.

Have the teenagers form four groups. Distribute a Bible and a mask to each group. Say: **Choose someone in your group to wear the mask. Then discuss what message the mask portrays.**

After several minutes of discussion, have groups choose new people to wear the masks. Ask groups to turn in their Bibles to Matthew 7:15. Tell groups that the mask-wearing students are to read the verse aloud. Their goal is to read the verse in a way that reflects the opposite message from the mask. For example, if a mask portrays a friendly cartoon character, the student might read the verse with a mean and unfriendly voice. If a mask portrays an action hero, the student might read the verse in a timid and frightened voice.

Then have groups trade masks, and choose different students to wear the masks. Ask those students to read aloud Matthew 7:16, again in a way that reflects the opposite of the mask. Have groups continue swapping the masks and choosing different students to wear the masks and read aloud verses 17 and 18.

Afterward, collect the masks. Ask a volunteer to read aloud Matthew 7:15-18 in his or her regular voice. Then have groups discuss these questions:

- **How do masks conceal us?**
- **What kinds of masks do people wear in life?**
- **How is the way we read the verses similar to the way false prophets function?**
- **What are some of the dangers of evaluating someone's message based on outward appearances?**
- **Based on the Scripture, what might be some better ways to evaluate someone's message?**

Say: **Each mask you wore today communicates a certain message. But when we read the verses, we communicated an entirely different message. In a similar way, people may use appearances to communicate that they are good, trustworthy, and caring. But it's what's underneath the skin that really matters. It's what they do that truly shows us who they are.**

The Big Picture

Theme: God's omniscience

Scripture: Isaiah 55:8-9

Supplies: You'll need pictures that show close-up details—perhaps from science books, maps, or personal photos—and corresponding pictures that show larger-scale views of the detailed photos. For example, you could use a road map that includes an inset of a downtown area, or you could use a family picture that was taken from a distance along with a close-up photo of one family member. Another idea would be to take a personal photo to a copy store and make an enlargement of one part of the photo.

Use this activity to illustrate God's ability to see the full picture of our lives while we can only see a small fragment at a time.

Gather students together, and ask:

- **How many of you have made plans that later didn't work out? Explain.**
- **Why do you think that happens?**

Ask a volunteer to read aloud Isaiah 55:8-9.

Say: **We're going to see what God means in this Scripture.**

Distribute the more detailed pictures, and have the students discuss what they see. Stimulate the discussion with questions such as "What do you think this person is doing?" or "What does this map tell you about the area?" After a couple of minutes, reveal the pictures of the larger scale views and ask students to again discuss what they see. Ask:

- **How did the information you gleaned from the first pictures compare to the information you gleaned from the second pictures?**
- **How do the detailed pictures represent our ability to see what's happening in our lives?**

• How do the larger-scale pictures represent God's ability to see what's happening in our lives?

Say: **We can only see the parts of our lives that we've already lived—and even some of those memories are distant. We seem to be most aware of the details surrounding what's happening in our lives *right now.* God, on the other hand, can see everything in our lives. Sometimes things don't work out the way we plan, but we can always take comfort in the fact that God can see the big picture of our lives.**

Building God's Kingdom

Theme: Unity
Scripture: Ephesians 2:19-22
Supplies: You'll need a Bible, a deck of playing cards, and clear tape.

This idea illustrates that we are all important parts of Christ's body and that if we work together, we can effectively build God's kingdom.

Distribute two or three cards to each person, and instruct students each to make a house of cards using only the cards given to them. Provide clear tape to help with construction.

After a few minutes, encourage teenagers to combine resources with a few people around them to make bigger houses. After a few more minutes, tell teenagers to combine all of their cards and work together to make one large house of cards.

Ask a volunteer to read aloud Ephesians 2:19-22.

Say: **Christianity becomes most effective when we join together as one body, working side by side to build Christ's kingdom instead of struggling individually with our limited resources. God has given each of us specific skills and strengths to build upon.** Ask:

• What types of problems cause division among Christians?

• How can Christians work through those issues?

• Have you ever been at odds with another Christian? Explain.

• How was the situation resolved?

To close the activity, spend several minutes affirming each student's strengths, naming specific abilities and talents students have used to build the group. For example, you could say, "Theresa, you did us all such a favor by organizing the publicity for the car wash. You really have a knack for getting people excited about events!"

Bump or Bless?

Theme: Speech

Scripture: 2 Corinthians 1:3-4

Supplies: You'll need a Bible, marbles, and masking tape.

Use this lesson to help students understand that their words should be used to build others up and to bless them.

Before the activity, use masking tape to create a circle on the floor. If you have more than six students, make a circle for every three or so students.

Give each student a marble. Invite teenagers to roll their marbles in the masking tape circle and try to knock other marbles out of the circle. Suggest that the group make and abide by its own rules.

After a few minutes of play, ask:

• What was fun about this game?

• What was it like to be bumped out of the circle? to bump others out of the circle?

• How were the marbles in our game similar to harsh words?

Say: **Even though we all want to be treated with care and compassion, we sometimes use words and actions to knock each other around.**

Invite a volunteer to read aloud 2 Corinthians 1:3-4. Ask:

• Why do we notice the comfort we receive more often than the comfort we give?

• Why might we want to become intentionally caring about the way we use our words?

• How can we become intentionally caring about the way we use our words?

• How will you use your words to bless people instead of bumping them?

Our words can be used powerfully to build up and encourage others or to do them great harm. We must bless others and not "bump" them with our words.

Caretakers of Creation

Theme: Creation

Scripture: Genesis 2:18-20; Psalm 84:1-4

Supplies: You'll need a Bible and a dog, a cat, or another pet that enjoys being around people.

This activity can be a fun way of teaching the diversity of God's creation and our need to care for God's creatures.

Bring the pet into the room as a surprise, and allow the teenagers to pet the animal. Once everyone has settled down, ask:

- **Why do you think we get so much joy out of animals?**
- **How might you feel about this animal if you had created it?**
- **How have human beings made the world a more difficult place for some animals to exist?**
- **What are some ways we can be better caretakers of God's creation?**

Read aloud Genesis 2:18-20, and then ask:

- **What insights did you receive from this passage about the relationship between people and animals?**

Read aloud Psalm 84:1-4. Ask:

- **How do animals like sparrows make our world a more beautiful place in which to worship God?**
- **How do the creatures God created enhance our understanding of God?**
- **How can we show God that we appreciate all the things he made?**

After the students have brainstormed ways to show their appreciation to God, have the group choose a few ideas to put into action. Say: **God made all the animals, including this pet, and said that they were good. Instead of disrespecting God's creative work, we can each help care for creation. In fact, let's start caring for God's creation right now.** Allow teenagers to enjoy the company of the pet for a while.

Catalyst for God

Theme: Faith

Scripture: Ephesians 2:8-9

Supplies: You'll need a Bible; a small, clear jar with a tight screw-on lid; water colored with five to ten drops of food coloring; vegetable oil; and a bottle of grease-cutting dish soap such as Dawn.

Use this lesson to help students understand how faith brings us closer to God.

Ask for three volunteers to help you with an experiment. Give one student the colored water, one the container of vegetable oil, and one the bottle of dish soap.

Tell the students that the colored water represents people. Ask the person holding the water to pour it into the empty jar, filling the jar halfway. Then tell the students that the vegetable oil represents God, and ask the student holding the vegetable oil to finish filling the jar with oil. The layers of water and oil will separate quickly, leaving two distinct layers. Have teenagers pass around the jar, and ask:

- **How does this experiment represent people's relationship with God?**
- **How can the separation between people and God be removed?**

After a few minutes of discussion, ask a volunteer to read aloud Ephesians 2:8-9. Then hold up the dish soap. Say: **This dish soap represents faith. Let's see what happens to our relationship with God when we add faith.** Have the student with the dish soap squeeze several drops of soap into the jar. Put the lid on tightly and shake the jar for about ten seconds. The layers of oil and colored water will mix into an evenly colored mixture. Have students pass around the jar again. Ask:

- **What does faith do for our relationship with God?**
- **How does this experiment represent the Scripture we read?**

Say: **Before we believe in God and his Son, Jesus, we are separated from God just as the water was separated from the oil. But faith—belief in God that leads us to give our lives to him—dissolves that barrier just as the dish soap dissolved the "barrier" between the oil and water.**

Chasing the Wind

Theme: Idle pursuits
Scripture: Ecclesiastes 2:1-11
Supplies: You'll need a Bible, an electric fan, and a bag of craft feathers (available at craft stores).

Use this lesson to help students understand the danger of chasing idle pursuits and pleasures rather than pursuing Jesus.

Set the electric fan on a table. Have teenagers form two teams.

Stand behind the fan, and have one person from each team stand about three feet in front of the fan. Hold up the feathers and explain: **When I let go of these feathers, your job is to catch as many as you can before they touch the floor. Once a feather lands on the floor, it is out of play. When all the feathers have either been caught or have landed on the floor, count the feathers you've caught.**

Turn on the fan, release the feathers, and let the two students chase them. After all the feathers have been caught or have fallen, turn off the fan. Have the students count the feathers they caught, pick up all the feathers, and return them. Then have two new players try, repeating the action until everyone has had a turn.

Afterward, have the teenagers sit down with their team members. Ask:

• **What do you think the phrase "chasing after the wind" means?**

Have a couple of volunteers share the job of reading aloud Ecclesiastes 2:1-11. Then have groups discuss these questions:

• **What are some of the pleasures people chase after in today's society?**

• **How is chasing after pleasure or wealth like chasing after these feathers in the wind?**

• **Have you ever tried to get something or do something that you thought you really wanted, only to discover that you weren't satisfied once you got it? Tell about that experience.**

• **What do you think really satisfies? How do you achieve it?**

• How can chasing after pleasure or wealth distract you from a satisfying relationship with Jesus Christ?

• If you were to name the one thing that is most likely to distract you from pursuing your relationship with Jesus, what would it be?

Give each person a feather to carry as a reminder of the futility of pursuing pleasure.

A Cord of Three Strands

Theme: Unity

Scripture: Ecclesiastes 4:12

Supplies: You'll need a Bible and, for each person, a marker and a strip of light-colored fabric that's approximately two inches wide and one foot long. Use several different, coordinating colors of fabric.

Use this idea to illustrate how we are stronger together than we are alone.

Give each person a marker and a strip of cloth. Say: **First write your name at the very end of your cloth. Then find something in the room to try to lift with your cloth. For example, you could loop your strip under the arm of a chair and try to lift the chair.**

Give students a few minutes to test the strength of their strips of cloth. Then say: **Now find two other people and braid your three strips together. When you've finished, test the strength of your combined strips of cloth by trying to pick up those same objects again.**

Circulate while students are working in case they need assistance. If your group is not divisible by three, have the students treat two strips or braids as one so that no one is left out.

After groups have tested the strength of their braids, say: **Now find two other groups and make a bigger braid out of your three group braids.** When students have completed the one large braid, have them test the strength of the braid again.

When the braid is complete, read aloud Ecclesiastes 4:12. Ask:

• How does the strength of our braid now compare to the strength of your single strip of cloth?

• How does our braid reflect what happens when people work together?

• In what ways are we stronger together than we are apart?

• How does the diversity of colors in this braid illustrate the diversity among God's people? in our group?

Have students get back in their original trios to discuss these questions:

• How do you see yourself in the "braid" of this group? For example, are you woven tightly in, or are you a loose strand?

• How can this group support and strengthen you in prayer this week?

Have students pray in their trios.

Display the braid in the classroom as a reminder of your group's unity and strength.

Dirty Clothes

Theme: Sin

Scripture: 2 Samuel 11:2-5, 14-15; Psalm 51:1-12

Supplies: You'll need a Bible and a hamper or laundry basket filled with obviously dirty laundry such as clothing or rags. Make sure you have at least one dirty item per person, and be sure only to include items that you don't mind your teenagers seeing.

Use this idea to remind your group of how awful sin is, how it collects if not taken care of, and how easily it can be cleansed from our lives.

Gather everyone in a circle, then dump out the dirty laundry in the middle of the circle. Distribute an article of clothing to each person. Have everyone get in groups of three or four and discuss how they think the item became dirty. After a few minutes of discussion, gather everyone back together. Ask:

• How are these dirty items like sin in our lives?

• How do you think these items became dirty?

• How is that like the different ways sin comes into our lives?

Read aloud 2 Samuel 11:2-5, 14-15. Ask:

• How are the consequences of not doing laundry like the consequences of not dealing with sin?

• Have you ever put something clean in with your dirty clothes? What happens?

Say: **David committed a second sin to cover up his first sin with Bathsheba. If we don't deal with sins immediately, they begin to pile up like dirty laundry. And sin is like mixing dirty and clean clothes—it stinks everything up.**

Explain that David wrote Psalm 51 after his sin was exposed. Read aloud Psalm 51:1-12. Say: **When we come before God to confess our sin, God removes our sin and makes us clean again.**

Do I Know You?

Theme: Relationship With Christ

Scripture: John 10:14

Supplies: You'll need a Bible, paper, pencils, and some pictures of people that the group knows and some pictures of people that the group may have seen or heard of but don't know personally. For example, include pictures of yourself, group members, and church members, plus pictures of movie stars or political figures.

Use this lesson to emphasize the importance of having a personal relationship with Jesus.

Lay the pictures in a random order on a table. Distribute paper and pencils, and ask youth to list the names of all the people. Then ask youth to write one thing they personally like about each person on their lists. After everyone has finished, ask:

- **How many of you know all of these people?**
- **What differences do you see on your lists between the people you personally know and the people you don't personally know?**
- **What are the differences in the relationships you have with the people you know and the people you don't know?**

Ask a volunteer to read aloud John 10:14. Say: **It's difficult to really know someone that you don't have a personal relationship with. It takes time to get to know someone and have personal relationship with him or her. The same goes with Jesus. You cannot know him if you're not spending time with him.**

Before ending the activity, have students discuss ways they can get to know Jesus more personally.

Eggsitement!

Theme: Unity

Scripture: Ephesians 4:3-6

Supplies: You'll need a Bible; a hard-boiled egg for each person; a big bowl; and egg decorating supplies such as paint pens, crayons, and stickers.

Use this lesson to illustrate how God can unite diverse Christians to accomplish wonderful things.

Have students sit in a circle. Place the hard-boiled eggs and decorating supplies in the middle of the group. Distribute an egg to each person.

Instruct teenagers to decorate the eggs to represent themselves. Encourage students to be creative and to include symbols of things that are important to them or words that describe how they're unique. Decorate an egg to represent yourself as well.

After about five minutes, go around the circle and allow everyone who wants to describe his or her egg to do so.

Then read aloud Ephesians 4:3-6. Say: **Paul encourages us to guard our unity as Christians and reminds us of several things that unify us.** Read aloud verses 4-5 again.

Next hold up your egg. Ask:

- **How do our eggs reflect our individual differences? our similarities?**
- **How might the differences cause conflicts?**
- **How might the similarities bring us together?**

Say: **These eggs reflect our individuality. Sometimes we're so different from one another that problems result. But underneath the surface, we're really more similar than different.** Have each person crack and peel the egg's shell and put the shell pieces into the bowl. Ask:

- **How do the shells reflect what happens when we have to give up some of our individuality?**
- **How does what's left of our eggs reflect our similarities?**

Say: **As Christians, we share many similarities—one body, one Spirit, one hope, one Lord, one faith, one baptism, one God and Father of all.**

Ask:

• Why is it sometimes difficult to blend yourself with other people?

• How can remembering our similarities make a difference in our relationships and work with one another?

Say: **We had to break the eggs in order to make them good to eat. In a similar way, we sometimes have to give up some of our individuality to blend with others. But when Christians come together, God can use us to accomplish wonderful things.**

Empty Promises

Theme: Living out faith

Scripture: James 2:14-17

Supplies: You'll need a Bible; food that comes in boxes such as crackers, doughnuts, and cookies; plastic containers; slips of paper; and a pen.

Use this lesson to join actions with the faith we profess.

Before the activity, take the food out of the boxes and place it in plastic containers. Then write on slips of paper, "Enjoy your food!" Place the slips of paper inside the empty food boxes.

Tell your students that you have snacks for everyone. Toss the boxes to several people. They'll figure out that the boxes are empty when they catch them. Have students open the boxes anyway to see what's inside. When teenagers have found the slips of paper, ask:

• What's your reaction to this statement?

• How would you feel about someone who gave you empty boxes when what you needed was something to eat?

Invite a volunteer to read aloud James 2:14-17, and then ask:

• How does our faith affect our desire to act?

• Do you know someone who is in

Extension Idea

If you wish, you could use this object lesson as a springboard for social or community service. As a group, brainstorm about needs in your community and ways you could work to meet those needs. For example, you could volunteer at a homeless shelter or a food pantry, or you could organize a coat drive for needy kids.

need? Don't think just of physical need; maybe you know someone who needs a friend or someone to sit with in the lunchroom or encouragement of some kind.

• What can you do this week to act upon your faith instead of offering the equivalent of empty boxes of food?

To make sure your students don't go home with stomach pangs after all this talk about food, serve the food that originally came in the boxes.

Faith for the Big and Little Things

Theme: Faith
Scripture: Psalm 33:6-7
Supplies: You'll need a Bible and some tree branches from trees in your area.

Use this idea to illustrate that faith is an act of will and that just as we trust the workings of the universe to God, we can trust our daily lives to him.

Give the tree branches to a few different young people, and instruct them to pass the branches around the group so everyone gets a chance to handle a branch.

Say: **Take a look at these branches we're passing around. They came from trees in this area. As you look at them, pay attention to what they say about the season of the year we're in right now.**

After kids have passed around the branches, ask:

• What do these branches say about the season we're in right now?

• If you didn't know what season it is, could you tell by looking at these tree branches? Why or why not?

• If left on the trees, what do you believe these branches will look like in six months?

• How do you know what the branches would look like in six months?

Say: **None of us knows for sure what the branches will look like in six months. But because of past experience, we have faith in what we believe will happen.**

Have group members form trios to answer the following questions. After each question, ask trios to share their answers with the rest of the large group. Ask:

- **What does it mean to have faith?**
- **When is it hard for you to have faith in God?**

Say: **Sometimes it seems hard to have faith. Sometimes we wonder if we even *have* any faith! But we often think of faith in a backward way. We think that faith depends on us rather than on God. We make faith more complicated than it needs to be.**

Ask:

- **Do you have faith that the sun will come up every morning? Why?**
- **If you don't have faith that the sun will come up, will it come up anyway?**
- **Do you have faith that the seasons will change every year? Why?**
- **Even if you don't have faith, will the seasons change anyway?**

Say: **So much of faith is just relying on the object of your faith rather than on your inward feelings of faith. Just as the sun is going to come up whether you believe it will or not, God is going to remain constant whether you believe in him or not.**

When you put your faith in God, that's all you have to do. Just rest in the fact that he's there and that he's taking care of you. You believe the sun will come up in the morning and that the seasons will change. You don't spend every night agonizing over whether you have enough faith to make the sun come up in the morning. You just trust God to make it happen. God can handle the workings of the whole universe, so can't you trust him to handle the details of your life?

Read aloud Psalm 33:6-7. Then have trios pray together that God will simplify and strengthen their faith.

Fearfully and Wonderfully Made

Theme: Self-esteem

Scripture: Psalm 139:1-12

Supplies: You'll need a Polaroid camera, or enough small hand mirrors for each person to have one, and a Bible.

This object lesson will help teenagers understand that God has a special plan for each of them.

Take a Polaroid picture of each student, or give each student a small hand mirror.

Have students look closely at the pictures or into the mirrors as you read Psalm 139:1-12 aloud. Ask them to reflect on God's plans for their lives as they listen. You may want to play some quiet music in the background. When you're finished, ask:

• **How did this exercise make you feel? Explain.**

• **How does it make you feel to realize that God knows you so intimately? Explain.**

Say: **God knows exactly who you are. He knows everything there is to know about you because he created you. You are each very precious and special to God, and he has wonderful plans for your life.**

Five Smooth Stones

Theme: God's protection
Scripture: 1 Samuel 17:40-50
Supplies: You'll need Bibles, markers, and five small stones for each person.

Use this idea to remind students that with God they can face any challenge.

Have youth form groups of four, and distribute Bibles, markers, and stones. Be sure each student has five stones. In their foursomes, have teenagers read 1 Samuel 17:40-50 (provide a brief background to the story if your students are unfamiliar with it) and discuss these questions:

• **Would you have gone against a giant with just five little stones? Explain.**

• **According to verse 45, what was David's real weapon?**

Say: **David said he came in the name of the Lord Almighty. Let's think of as many names for God as we can—for example, "Good Shepherd," "Heavenly Father," "King of Kings." As you hear a name that is especially meaningful to you, write it on one of your stones. If it won't fit, draw a symbol to remind you of the name.**

After the group has mentioned several names for God, have people get back into their foursomes to discuss these questions:

• **What names did you choose? Why did you choose them?**

• What challenging or threatening situation are you facing in your life right now?

• Which of the names of God on your stones gives you the most comfort as you think about that situation? Explain.

• How can you experience God's power in that situation?

Encourage the teenagers to place their five smooth stones where they can see or touch them as they face their challenges.

For What It's Worth

Theme: Needs vs. luxuries

Scripture: Matthew 25:21

Supplies: You'll need nine items, such as a telephone, a bag of rice, tennis shoes, a remote control, an order of french fries, a jacket, car keys, a computer mouse, and a bottle of water.

Use this activity to encourage students to see themselves as one of God's most valuable resources.

Have students form nine groups, and give each group one of the items in the supply list. If you have a smaller class, you may want to give some groups two items. Ask group members to discuss whether the item they have is either a luxury or a need based on these questions:

• Could you go without using or eating this item for an entire week? Why or why not?

• What makes some of them crucial and others not so crucial to our lives?

• Which of these items do you think God gives us as resources? Why?

Have groups share with the class how they determined whether their items are luxuries or needs. Say: **God doesn't necessarily want us to get rid of things we might consider a luxury, but it's important to understand the difference between needs and luxuries. All these things are gifts from God. Everything we have belongs to God. We should be thankful, but not demand that God give us what we want. Instead, we should focus on how to faithfully and responsibly use the resources God gives us.**

Read Matthew 5:21.

Then ask:

• **What are some resources God has given us that we can use for him?**

• **How can we learn to more faithfully use resources God gives us for his work?**

• **How can we be more thankful for the gifts and resources God gives us?**

Say: **Let's be thankful for what God gives us, understanding that they're gifts. We don't deserve them, and we shouldn't demand them. We should joyfully and faithfully use what we are given by him to do his work.**

From the Heart

Theme: Relationship with Christ
Scripture: John 14:21
Supplies: You'll need a Bible, red construction paper, pens, and scissors.

Use this idea to help group members see that obeying God can be even more of a fulfilling, joyful experience.

Distribute a pen and a sheet of red construction paper to each person. Have scissors available. Have each person fold a sheet of red construction paper in half vertically. Demonstrate how to draw half a heart shape on the fold of the paper, cut on the line, then open the paper to reveal a full heart.

Say: **Think of someone you barely know. On the left side of your heart, write a few lines to describe that relationship. For example, you might say that you would never call that person if you were upset, or that you don't really know or care what that person thinks of you.**

Give participants a few minutes to write, then ask volunteers to share what they wrote.

Say: **Now think of someone you really care about—a best friend or a boyfriend or girlfriend. On the right side of your heart, describe that relationship. You might say that you would put that person's wishes before your own, or that you would never doubt that person's loyalty.**

After a few minutes, ask volunteers to share what they wrote. Then ask:

• **How is a distant acquaintance different from a close relationship?**

• **Which kind of relationship is more important to you? Why?**

• If you met someone and progressed from an acquaintance to a close relationship, would you ever want to go back to being distant with each other? Explain.

Read aloud John 14:21. Say: **This verse points out that the more we love Jesus, the more we'll know what he wants and we'll do what he wants. Following Jesus' commands is evidence that we really know him.**

Ask:

• How can we get to know Jesus better?

• What kind of commands is this verse referring to?

• Why do you think following Jesus' commands is evidence of a close, loving relationship with him?

Say: **As we grow in our relationship with Jesus, we'll understand more what he wants from us. And we'll love him more. Let's follow Jesus to show that we love him.**

God Is My Rock

Theme: God's protection

Scripture: 2 Samuel 22:2-3

Supplies: You'll need a Bible; a lot of rocks (at least one for each person); a large stack of any kind of paper; and a bunch of fabric, such as blankets, sheets, and towels.

Use this lesson to remind teenagers that God always has been and always will be their stronghold.

Have youth form three groups, and give one group a lot of rocks. Give another group a large stack of paper. Give the third group a bunch of fabric, such as blankets, sheets, and towels. Have each group use its building material to create a wall. After five minutes, have all the groups show the walls they've created. Ask:

• **If our groups were going to attack one another, which building material would you want to have for your wall: paper, rocks, or fabric? Why?**

• **Which material could make the strongest, safest wall?**

• **How is God like a rock?**

• **How is the wall of rocks like the wall we stand behind when we trust in God?**

Have a volunteer read aloud 2 Samuel 22:2-3. Say: **Different names for God give us clear pictures of who God is. God is a rock, a fortress, a deliverer, a shield, and the horn of salvation, so we can always depend on him.** Have students each take home a rock as a reminder of God's protection.

Extension Idea

Allow students to go outside to find other objects that represent God's protection and provision. Then have students come back inside, show what they found, and tell how the objects represent God's protection. For example, a student may collect some water from a puddle and say, "Water reminds me of God's protection because water gives us strength, and God gives us the strength we need to stand against our enemies."

God Talk

Theme: Prayer

Scripture: Matthew 6:9-13

Supplies: You'll need a Bible, a pager, a computer with e-mail, a cellular phone, a telephone, paper, pens, chalkboard or dry-erase board, and chalk or a dry-erase marker.

Use this lesson to emphasize the importance of prayer in our lives with God.

Before the activity, arrange to have someone call your pager during the object lesson. You could have an adult volunteer plan to slip out of the classroom at your signal and call your pager. A pager that signals with a sound would be most effective.

To begin, show students the various communication devices in the room. Invite the students to use them to demonstrate some ways they most commonly communicate with friends. While students are demonstrating, signal your volunteer to call your pager.

After the pager has sounded, say: **Every day you and I communicate with many people. We do this over the telephone, through computers, and with face-to-face conversations. Many of you even have pagers to help you keep in touch with people who might want to reach you. Obviously, communication is**

Extension Idea

Copy on paper the ideas about how youth can be in touch with God every day, and give each teenager a copy. You could also include a guide to prayer or other helpful resources they can use to improve their prayer lives.

very important to us. We even make sure other people can reach us no matter where we are.

Ask:

• Why, then, do you think it can be so difficult for us to spend time talking to God?

Allow volunteers to offer reasons for our reluctance to speak with God. Ask a volunteer to write the responses on the eraser board. Ask:

• Why do you think it might be important for us to talk to God?

Allow volunteers to offer reasons it might be important to speak with God. Ask a volunteer to write the responses on the eraser board.

Invite someone to read aloud Matthew 6:9-13. Then say: **Jesus thought prayer was important. He often spent time talking with his Father, and in this Scripture passage, he taught his followers how to pray.**

You and I have opportunities each day to spend time communicating with God just as we communicate with others. But we don't need a pager to reach God. All we have to do is speak to him as we would a father or friend. This is called prayer.

Ask:

• How might we learn to pray each day?

• What are some helpful ways to be in touch with God each day?

Again, ask a volunteer to write students' ideas on the eraser board. Then give teenagers a couple of minutes to pray to God.

God's Flashlight

Theme: God's Word

Scripture: Psalm 119:105; 2 Timothy 3:16

Supplies: You'll need a Bible, and enough flashlights and index cards for every four to six people to have one of each.

Use this idea to remind your group that God's Word will control their thoughts and actions every day if they keep it in their hearts.

Before the activity, write out Psalm 119:105 and 2 Timothy 3:16 on each index card.

Have youth form groups of four to six. Distribute a flashlight to each group. Darken the room completely, then distribute the index cards. First have groups attempt to read the verses in the darkness. Then allow groups to use their flashlights to read the verses. Ask groups to discuss these questions:

- **What do these verses say is the purpose of God's Word?**
- **What's it like to be surrounded by darkness?**
- **How was trying to read the verses in the darkness like trying to live without the help of God's Word?**
- **How can knowing what God's Word says give you light when you feel surrounded by the darkness of fear? worry? doubt? stress? sin?**

Turn on the lights. Hold up a Bible, and say: **God gave us the Bible as a guiding light—kind of like a flashlight. And God expects us to use that light, to follow it in our daily lives, to let it control our thoughts and actions. Sometimes Scripture teaches and trains, and sometimes it rebukes and corrects. It always provides a light for our path. Just as a flashlight has to be turned on to be useful, we must know what God's Word says—we must hide it in our hearts—if we want it to control our thoughts and actions.**

Going Through the Trash

Theme: Creation

Scripture: Colossians 1:16

Supplies: You'll need a Bible; a trash bag full of trash—the nastier the better; a small, sealed container of cookies placed inside the trash bag (be sure to wrap the cookies well); and plastic or rubber gloves.

Use this lesson to illustrate the importance of caring for the earth God has given us.

Bring in a bag of smelly, nasty trash, and tell the youth there is a surprise somewhere in the bag of trash. Ask for the group to sift through the trash to find the prize. Really encourage the group to seek the present, telling them it will be worth the effort.

If you have volunteers, have them go through the trash until they find the

container of cookies. Then set aside the container, and allow the volunteers to wash their hands.

If you don't have any volunteers, distribute plastic or rubber gloves and see if that helps your recruitment. But even if no one volunteers, it's OK—the object lesson will still work. No matter what, discuss these questions:

• **Why were you hesitant to go through the trash even though you knew it contained something special for you?**

• **What makes the trash so unappealing?**

• **Can you think of a time you were at a park or a lake or somewhere similar that had a lot of trash? Describe it for us.** To get students started, you may want to talk about a time you've been someplace that had been trashed by people.

• **How is seeing God's creation covered in trash similar to our activity?**

Extension Idea

Have students choose an area—either the church grounds or someplace close by—to clear of trash regularly. You could even distribute trash bags and have the group get started just after this object lesson.

If no volunteers offered to find the treat in the trash, put on a rubber glove and find the container of cookies in the trash bag. Pass around the cookies so everyone gets one. Ask a volunteer to read aloud Colossians 1:16. Ask:

• **How do you think God feels when we mess up these things that were created by him and for him—his creation?**

• **What can we do to help take care of God's creation?**

Say: **I think you will all agree that it's important for us to take care of this incredible earth God has given us. We can do that by throwing our trash in a container or by recycling or by helping to clean up when others make a mess.**

Good Fortune

Theme: Future
Scripture: Jeremiah 29:11
Supplies: You'll need a Bible, and a fortune cookie for each person. You can buy fortune cookies at grocery stores or Chinese restaurants.

Use this activity to introduce the idea that leaving our future to God is the best path to success.

Have youth form groups of four, and distribute a fortune cookie to each person. Have students eat their cookies and read the fortunes inside.

Instruct students to discuss their fortunes with one another and match their fortunes with the people in the group they think the fortunes most describe now or will most describe in the future.

Then gather everyone back together, and ask:

• **What kind of advice is available to you regarding what to do with your future?**

• **How do you choose which advice to listen to?**

• **Why do you think so many people consult psychics, tarot cards, fortunetellers, palm readers, and the like to find their future?**

Read aloud Jeremiah 29:11. Ask:

• **Why do you think it makes sense to consult God for our future?**

Say: **Most of us would like to know what the future holds or would like someone to tell us what choices we should make to get to where we would like to be. But God is the only one who truly knows the future, and he has plans for us. We can trust our future to God because he promises to prosper us, give us hope, and give us a future. What a good fortune to have!**

Good Friends

Theme: Friendship
Scripture: Proverbs 17:17; 18:24
Supplies: You'll need a Bible, and one balloon for every two people.

Use this lesson to emphasize the importance of friendship in difficult times.

Have youth form pairs. Ask a volunteer to read aloud Proverbs 17:17. Say: **There are few things in the world as special as good friends. They can help you in all kinds of situations. But a true friend loves at all times, even during adversity.**

Ask the pairs to join right or left hands. Tell pairs that their task is to blow up and tie off the balloon without letting go of each other's joined hands. Encourage partners to work together to get the job done. After they have completed the task, ask:

• How did you work together to blow up the balloon in this difficult activity?

• How was working together on this difficult activity like sticking with a friend during a difficult time?

• What are the typical characteristics of a friend that will stick with you during difficult times?

Read aloud Proverbs 18:24. Say: **Good friends stick together. Blowing up and tying off a balloon while holding hands is a difficult task. But isn't it wonderful when our good friends stick with us during difficult times?**

Good Measure

Theme: Generosity

Scripture: Luke 6:38

Supplies: You'll need a Bible, M&M's or other small candies, and a measuring cup or spoon for each person.

Use this idea to illustrate generosity.

Have teenagers form pairs, and say: **We're going to enjoy a snack now. One partner will give the other partner his or her serving. That means the first partner will determine how much candy the second partner will get.**

Set out the candy and measuring cups or spoons, and instruct the first partners to dole out the candy. Then have partners reverse roles so the second partners dole out candy to the first partners. Afterward, ask:

• How did you decide how much candy to give to your partner?

• How do you react when someone gives generously to you? when someone gives stingily to you?

Ask a volunteer to read aloud Luke 6:38. Then walk around the room and give each student an amount of candy similar to the amount of candy they each gave to their partner.

Then have partners discuss these questions:

• Do you think it's true that we get back a measure similar to what we give? Explain.

• Based on this verse, how do you think God responds to stinginess or selfishness? to generosity?

• Does this verse promise that God will return to you exactly the amount that you give away? Explain.

• What are some ways God rewards generosity?

• On a scale of one teaspoon to one gallon, what kind of a giver would you say you are?

• What kind of giver would you like to be?

• What is keeping you from giving as generously as you would like?

Have partners close the activity by praying together, asking God for generous hearts.

The Great Cover-Up

Theme: God's omniscience

Scripture: Hebrews 4:13

Supplies: You'll need a Bible and a bag filled with enough cosmetic items—pimple cream, mascara, lipstick, foundation, and so on—for every two to four people to have at least one.

Use this idea to discuss how we try to hide our faults or imperfections from others, and how we cannot hide anything from God.

Have teenagers form groups of two to four, and distribute at least one cosmetic item to each group. Have group members discuss the function of each item—specifically what that item is supposed to hide or reveal.

After a minute or two, gather everyone together, and have groups share their items and the items' functions. Then ask the whole group to discuss these questions:

• What are some things about our external selves that people try to hide? How do we hide? Why do we hide?

• What are some things about our internal selves that we try to hide?

Extension Idea

For added fun, have group members actually use the cosmetic items. For example, each group could choose one group member on whom to put the cosmetics. If you choose to do this, include discussion questions such as "How well do the cosmetics hide people's true features?" and "How is that like what happens when we try to hide our faults from each other? from God?"

How do we hide? Why do we hide?

Ask a volunteer to read aloud Hebrews 4:13. Ask:

• **How have you tried to hide things from God?**

• **How does it make you feel to know that God knows everything about you?**

Say: **We might succeed sometimes in hiding things from others, but we will never hide anything from God. Everything we are and everything we do is laid bare before God's eyes. That might seem scary, but it can also be comforting. Even though God knows everything about us—even the faults we try most desperately to hide—God loves us! No matter what, God's love for us doesn't change.**

Health Food

Theme: Spiritual health
Scripture: John 6:35; 1 Timothy 4:8
Supplies: You'll need a Bible, candy bars, a knife, and health-food energy bars.

Use this object lesson to illustrate the importance of seeking spiritual strength.

To begin, slice up the two types of bars so each student can sample a piece of each. After students have tasted each type of bar, ask:

• **Which of these bars do you think is the best for your body? Why?**

• **How do you think each of these bars would make you feel if you ate them in large quantities?**

• **Why is what we eat important to our physical well-being?**

• **Which kind of bar do you eat most often? Why?**

Gather the group in a circle and ask volunteers to read aloud John 6:35 and 1 Timothy 4:8. Then ask:

• **What do these Scriptures tell you about our spiritual needs?**

• **What are you feeding your soul most often? Why?**

• **How do you think we receive spiritual nourishment?**

• What are some ways we can discover a deeper faith and a closer relationship with Jesus, who is the bread of life?

Say: **Just as the food we eat has an effect on our physical health, the spiritual food we eat has an effect on our spiritual health. When we seek spiritual nourishment from God's Word and from Jesus, the bread of life, our spiritual appetites are satisfied.**

Close by praying for the spiritual health of everyone in the group.

Help Each Other Rebuild

Theme: Compassion
Scripture: Romans 12:9-16
Supplies: You'll need a Bible and toy construction sets such as Lincoln Logs, Tinkertoys, blocks, or Legos.

Use this lesson to emphasize the importance of staying close to friends who have suffered pain or tragedy.

Divide the pieces of a construction set equally among youth, and ask them to construct creations that represent a time when they experienced hurt. As teenagers work, talk quietly with a couple of individuals, asking them if you can knock down their structures in a few minutes to illustrate a point.

When everyone has finished building, admire each person's work with a specific compliment. Then knock down the structures of the students you spoke with earlier. Say: **When people are hurting, they need compassion. Sadly, we often choose to ignore the needs of those around us, rejecting their hurt and showing insensitivity to their feelings. Whether we actively hurt others or just ignore their needs, the result is the same.**

Ask:

Extension Idea

Use this object lesson as part of a lesson on grief. As another part of the lesson, take your group to a funeral home when services aren't being held so the funeral director can teach teenagers how to visit during a funeral.

Extension Idea

Have your students brainstorm for fifty practical ways to help people who are suffering—those in the hospital or those who've lost their jobs, for example.

• What kinds of responses might be more Christlike?

Ask a volunteer to read aloud Romans 12:9-16. Then prompt the group to help those with broken structures to rebuild them. Ask:

• How does compassion affect people?

• What would you want someone to do for you if you were suffering?

• According to the Scripture, how else can you help others rebuild?

Give each student a building block to remind them to help friends rebuild after tragedies.

How May I Serve You?

Theme: Servanthood

Scripture: John 13:5-17

Supplies: You'll need a Bible, cups, hot chocolate if it's cold outside or cold lemonade if it's hot outside.

Use this activity to help your youth understand what it means to be a humble servant.

As students arrive, stop each person at the door to take his or her coat and other things. Show each student to a seat, and hang up the coats carefully.

After everyone has arrived, personally serve each person a beverage; pour one drink, and deliver the drink personally to a student before getting another student a drink. Behave in a quiet, gentle way throughout this process. When everyone has received a drink, ask:

• What did you think about my actions as you arrived today?

• What was it like to be served?

Ask a couple of volunteers to share the job of reading aloud John 13:5-17. Say: **The job of washing feet was left to the lowest of slaves. Think about it. They didn't have paved roads or tennis shoes in those days. When they walked into a house, they had very dirty feet. So a servant would wash the guests' feet.**

Ask:

• Why did Jesus wash the disciples' feet?

• What was Jesus trying to teach us when he washed the disciples' feet?

• What kinds of things do people do today that are similar to washing feet?

• What are some ways Christians today can be the kind of servant Jesus was during his time on earth?

Ask students to form pairs. Have pairs talk together about what they can do for each other to practice behaving as servants. For example, a student may commit to washing his partner's car, or a student may affirm her partner by describing how her partner has helped others.

After a few minutes, call everyone back together. Ask:

• What's your reaction to this taste of servanthood?

• How can you serve people outside our group in a similar way?

• What's the difference between an *act* of servanthood and an *attitude* of servanthood?

• How would you define an attitude of servanthood—what does it look like?

• How can your attitude toward others reflect the attitude Christ displayed as he washed his disciples' feet?

Say: **While servanthood certainly can be manifested in acts of kindness, it's more than that. It's an attitude of seeing others as worthy and of seeking to meet others' needs. If the Lord humbled himself to wash his disciples' feet as an example for us, how can we *not* humble ourselves to serve in whatever way Jesus needs us?**

If the Shoe Doesn't Fit

Theme: Judging

Scripture: Matthew 7:1-2

Supplies: You'll need a Bible and one pair of shoes of any style that are either way too big or way too small for you to wear.

Use this idea to help teenagers evaluate how quickly we judge others and whether it's right or wrong to do so.

Have your group members mix so that people of various heights are standing side by side in a circle. Then have them sit down, take off their shoes, and pass them to the person on their right. Have everyone attempt to put on the shoes that were handed to them, stand, and walk around the room. For some this may be simple, but for others it will be very difficult. Tell students that if they'll stretch

out or otherwise damage the shoes, they should not stand and walk around the room.

After a couple of minutes, gather everyone back together. Ask:

• Why was it easy or difficult for you to walk in someone else's shoes?

• Have you ever had to wear a pair of shoes that were too big or too tight? What happened?

Hold up the pair of shoes you brought to the meeting. Ask:

• If I had to walk a mile in these shoes, what do you think would happen to my feet?

Read aloud Matthew 7:1-2. Say: **When we are tempted to judge someone, we must remind ourselves that we lack facts and usually do not know the whole story or the perspectives of the people involved. We must also "wear the other person's shoes," and put ourselves in their place and consider how they would feel to be judged. In fact, the Bible tells us that if we do judge others, we'll be judged in the same way. So if the shoe doesn't fit, don't wear it!**

Imitate Me

Theme: Living out faith
Scripture: Ephesians 5:1-2
Supplies: You'll need a Bible.

Use this idea to show teenagers that God wants us to imitate him in everything we do.

Have students form pairs, and have each pair choose one partner to be the initiator and one to be the imitator. Have partners stand face to face. Have the initiators—without speaking—make motions and facial expressions, and have each imitator try to mimic his or her initiator's motions and expressions exactly. After about a minute, have partners switch roles and try the exercise again. Afterward, ask:

• What was it like to try to imitate someone else's motions and expressions?

• What would it be like to try to imitate everything someone else did or said?

Read aloud Ephesians 5:1-2, and ask:

• What would your life be like if you imitated God constantly? Explain.

• In what areas of your life would you like to try to imitate God more closely? Explain.

Say: **The first step to becoming an imitator of God is to find out what God is like. We can do this through spending time reading God's Word, praying, and talking with other Christians. Let's all take a step this week to get to know God better.**

In the Womb

Theme: God's love
Scripture: Psalm 139:13-16
Supplies: You'll need a Bible, a videotape of an ultrasound, a TV, a VCR, paper, and markers.

Use this idea to demonstrate God's love in creating us.

Begin by having students discuss the following questions:

• Would you change anything about yourself if you could? Explain.

• How does God show you he cares about you?

• Do you ever wonder if God cares? Why?

Say: **Sometimes we wonder if God really cares about us. But we are reminded in the Bible that God does and always has cared about us. He cares about the details of our lives.**

Have a volunteer read aloud Psalm 139:13-16. Then turn on the videotape of the ultrasound, and allow teenagers to watch it for a few minutes. Ask them to describe what they see, point out features, and respond to the image of the baby in the womb.

Say: **Just as God created the child you're watching in his or her mother's womb, God created you. He put together every facet of your**

Extension Idea

Invite a pregnant woman to join you during this object lesson. Allow the students to touch her stomach and feel the child kicking and moving around. Ask the woman to tell the students about the baby's development, and then ask her what it's like for her to know that God created her child, knows her child, and loves her child.

being in your mother's womb. Even then, God knew you completely and loved you.

Give each person paper and a marker, and instruct kids to draw their own "ultrasounds" of themselves, pointing out unique features of their bodies and personalities. Encourage kids to be creative as they draw.

When kids are finished, allow volunteers to show what they drew. Ask:

• What does it mean to you that God created you, has always known you, and has always loved you?

• Earlier I asked you if you could change anything about yourself. Does your answer change based on the reminder that God created you, knows you, and loves you?

Have students spend a few moments in prayer, responding to God for creating them, knowing them, and loving them.

Is It Time Yet?

Theme: God's omniscience

Scripture: Ecclesiastes 3:1-8

Supplies: You'll need a Bible and several methods of keeping time, such as a small alarm clock, a watch, a kitchen timer, and a calendar.

Use this idea to help students understand that God has planned for things to occur in their own time.

Have students form as many groups as you have timepieces, and give each group a timepiece. Give groups thirty seconds to think of as many different ways as possible that their timepieces can be helpful to people. Then have groups share a few of their ideas. Ask:

• Why do we need to keep time?

• Have you ever been late for something? Explain.

• Do you think God is ever late? Why or why not?

Ask a volunteer to read aloud Ecclesiastes 3:1-8. Say: **This passage tells us that there is a time for everything that happens—both good things and bad things. We may not always understand God's timing; in fact, God's timing may seem to be off to us at times. But we can always trust that God sees the big picture; his timing is right and perfect.**

Keeping Your Balance

Theme: Living out faith

Scripture: Matthew 7:13-14

Supplies: You'll need a Bible and access to at least one narrow curb outside for group members to walk on. Another option would be to create one or more masking-tape trails inside that are only about three inches wide, or you could place a wooden 2x4 flat on the floor in your meeting area.

Use this activity to discuss the importance of staying on the narrow road spiritually, and the fact that it won't always be easy.

Have students get into groups of three. Have one member of each group walk on the curb or masking-tape trail without stepping off while the remaining two act as spotters on either side. If more than one curb or masking-tape trail is available, more than one group can be doing this at one time. Groups waiting their turn should act as cheerleaders for the balancing people. After everyone in all groups have had a chance to walk the curb or trail, gather everyone together in a circle. Ask:

- **What made balancing difficult or easy for you? What were some of the distractions?**
- **How do spotters help you balance?**
- **How do cheers and encouragement help you complete tasks?**

Read aloud Matthew 7:13-14. Ask:

- **Why is it sometimes difficult to stay on the narrow road spiritually?**
- **What are some of the distractions to living for God daily?**
- **How can we help one another find and stay on the narrow road that leads to life?**
- **How have others acted as spotters or cheerleaders in helping you live out your faith?**

Say: **Just as we're in danger of losing our balance in the physical world, we're in danger of losing our balance in the spiritual world. It can be difficult to stay on that narrow road. But just as the spotters helped you maintain your balance and the cheerleaders encouraged you, other Christians can help and encourage you in your spiritual walk.**

Known by Your Fruit

Theme: Living out faith

Scripture: Luke 6:43-45

Supplies: You'll need a Bible, paper, pens or pencils, several different kinds of leaves, and several different kinds of fruit. If you can get leaves for each kind of fruit (for example, pear tree leaves and a pear), that would be ideal.

Use this idea to illustrate how our actions identify what kind of people we are.

Set out each variety of leaf on a separate sheet of paper, and number each paper. Have students form groups of four, and give each group paper and a pen or pencil. Give group members a few minutes to examine the leaves, confer with each other, and write down what kinds of trees they think the leaves come from. Then ask the following questions, but make sure people don't tell what the leaves are yet:

• **How confident are you of your identifications? Explain.**

• **Which leaf is most difficult for you to identify?**

Next put each fruit by the leaf it matches (or if the fruit doesn't match the leaves, put out each piece of fruit on its own numbered page), and have the foursomes identify them.

Have foursomes report their conclusions. Then read aloud Luke 6:43-45, and have groups discuss these questions:

• **Are you more confident in identifying a tree by its leaves or its fruit? Explain.**

• **What do you think Jesus means by "fruit" in this Scripture?**

• **How does that kind of fruit show what kind of a person you are?**

• **How sure can you be whether or not someone is a Christian by observing how that person acts? Why or why not?**

• **What are some of the "leaves"—external appearances—that people use to identify or label others? How valid do you think those identifications are?**

• **If someone were to identify you by your "fruit," what do you think they would say about you?**

Say: **The closer we are to Jesus, and the more we love him, the more his fruit shows in our lives.**

Lay Down Your Burdens

Theme: Burdens
Scripture: Psalm 55:22; 1 Peter 5:6-7
Supplies: You'll need a Bible and six large balloons in the following colors: one blue, one green, two red, one black, and one white.

Use this object lesson to show teenagers that they must surrender their negative emotions to Christ to experience his peace and joy most fully.

Have students stand in a circle. Ask:

• **Have you ever been in a situation in which negative emotions kept you from feeling peace and joy? Explain.**

Ask a volunteer to help you. Say: **I'd like you to think about a difficult situation you've been in. Maybe it was a time you felt left out. When you feel left out, the first emotion you might feel is sadness. You might feel blue.** Hand the blue balloon to your volunteer. **When you feel blue, you might decide to pull away a bit from other people. Then when you see other people having a good time while you're not, you might feel a little jealous of them. You might be green with envy.** Hand the green balloon to your volunteer. **As you continue to see others having fun without you, you might start to feel angry. You might start to see red.** Hand one red balloon to your volunteer. **The angry feelings you're having now might remind you of other, older anger you have—such as anger at parents for getting divorced or anger at a brother or sister who gets better grades than you.** Hand the black balloon to your volunteer. **In your anger, you might choose to lash out at someone.** Bop the volunteer with the second red balloon, and then hand the balloon to him or her. **When you're in this angry state at past injustices, it can be difficult to experience the peace and power of Christ.**

Try to hand the white balloon to the volunteer. He or she probably will have a difficult time holding onto all the balloons at once.

Say: **The way you can fully experience the wonderful message of Christ's love is by offering to Christ the rest of your problems first.**

Have the volunteer hand all the balloons except the white one to the next person in the circle. Then have the volunteer give the person the white balloon. The person should then hand all the balloons but the white one to the next person in the circle. Have youth repeat this action until everyone has had a chance to hold all the balloons together and hold the white one alone.

Ask another volunteer to read aloud Psalm 55:22, then another to read 1 Peter 5:6-7. Say: **Jesus wants us to share everything with him—the good things and the bad things. If we give our negative emotions to him, we'll be able to experience his peace more fully.**

Ask:

• **Can you think of some negative things you'd like to share with Jesus?**

Say: **Let's have a moment of silent prayer. Spend some time asking Jesus to take from you the negative things you feel so that you'll be able to fully experience his peace.**

A Legacy of Love

Theme: Love

Scripture: John 13:35

Supplies: You'll need Bible and, for each person, a large index card and a pen. If available, bring your junior high or high school yearbook to display. Finally, you'll need to write the following poem on an eraser board:

Farewell, container of four years,
Full of my laughter, joy, and tears.
I smile, but inside no one sees
That all that's left is memories.
God, in the future may my name
Be associated not with beauty or fame
But with your love for all I met
Until the time for me you've set.
—Katrina Arbuckle

Use this lesson to emphasize the importance of sharing their love for one another.

Have students sit in a circle, and give each person an index card and a pen. Have teenagers write their names at the top of their cards. Then have students pass their cards around the circle so each person has a chance to sign a note on each index card as if signing a yearbook. Encourage teenagers to mention something they'll remember about each person.

When everyone gets his or her card back, give youth a few minutes to read the messages.

If your own yearbook is available, encourage everyone to look up your picture and read your classmates' messages.

After everyone has finished reading and looking, ask:

• **What kinds of messages did you receive? Did they surprise you? Why or why not?**

• **Years from now, how do you think people will remember you? Why?**

• **How would you most like to be remembered? Why?**

Point out the poem you wrote on the eraser board. Allow a minute or two for everyone to read the poem, then ask:

• **Why is it so important for us to be remembered?**

• **Do the things you'll be remembered for point to God being in your life? Why or why not?**

Read aloud John 13:35. Say: **If we're Christians, the one thing that should characterize us the most is love. Jesus said that if we love one another, others would know that we are his disciples. What a way to be remembered!**

Have students take home their index cards.

Extension Idea

Instead of having youth write messages on index cards, have them create a group yearbook. Bring in a Polaroid camera to take pictures of everyone. Then tape the photos to paper (one or two per page) and staple the pages together. Have everyone pass around the "yearbook" and write messages to each student beside his or her picture.

Lemonade Anyone?

Theme: Cheating

Scripture: Proverbs 16:11; 20:23

Supplies: You'll need a Bible, cold lemonade, plastic cups, and a pitcher of water.

Use this lesson to emphasize to students how God detests cheating.

Place the cups in a line on a table. Pour lemonade in each cup, but fill up the cups only halfway. Ask the youth to taste the lemonade. Instruct them to only take a small taste. Encourage them to comment on how they like the lemonade. Talk about how sweet it is and how cold. You might even have them talk about the times they enjoy lemonade the best. After everyone has had a chance to taste the lemonade, have them sit down.

As the youth are watching, fill the lemonade cups with water. Make sure the cups are almost full. Now ask the youth to taste the lemonade. Again, encourage them to comment on how they like the drink. Ask:

- **How does the lemonade taste now compared to the way it tasted before?**
- **How is watering down lemonade like cheating?**

Ask a volunteer to read aloud Proverbs 16:11, then another volunteer to read aloud Proverbs 20:23. Ask:

- **What's the difference between watered down lemonade and honest scales?**
- **What do these passages say about God's view of cheating?**

Say: **When we cheat, we may fool others, but we can't fool God. Honesty is as refreshing to God and to those around us as fresh lemonade on a hot summer day!** Give students a drink of regular strength lemonade.

Love at First Sight

Theme: Love

Scripture: Romans 15:7

Supplies: You'll need a Bible. You'll also need two volunteers who the group won't recognize (perhaps teenagers from another church's youth group). One should dress up in cool, stylish clothes, and the other should dress in shabby and out-of-style clothing.

Use this lesson to emphasize for students the importance of not showing favoritism in love.

Before this activity, be sure the volunteers know their roles.

Before a scheduled activity with your youth, have your volunteers arrive and mingle with the group. When class begins, introduce the volunteers to the group. Ask the volunteers to share how (and if) they were greeted earlier. Ask:

• How were the responses of group members to these people different? Explain.

• How would many people treat these two visitors differently? Why?

• What are some ways we can be sure to respond to all people with the same love, no matter how they look?

Ask a volunteer to read aloud Romans 15:7 to the group. Ask:

• How does accepting each other bring praise to God?

• What could we do to welcome people no matter how they look?

Say: **Christ accepts us for who we are. Shouldn't we do the same?**

The M&M's Theory

Theme: God's love
Scripture: 1 Samuel 16:7
Supplies: You'll need a Bible and enough M&M's candies for each student to have a small handful.

Use this lesson to emphasize to students the importance of not judging people by their outward appearance.

Distribute a small handful of M&M's candies to each person, but tell youth not to eat the candies yet. Ask:

• Which is your favorite color of M&M's?

• What makes that color better than the others?

Say: **Let's do a little experiment. Everybody find a green M&M.** Encourage teenagers to share with others until everyone has a green M&M. **We're going to eat this green M&M, and I want you all to concentrate on how it tastes. Ready?**

Have everyone eat his or her green M&M. Then ask the youth to describe what it tastes like. Allow several people to describe the flavor.

Once you have a good description of what a green M&M tastes like, ask everybody to find a yellow M&M. Make sure everyone has a yellow M&M. Then have youth eat the yellow M&Ms, focusing on the flavor. Then ask:

• How does a yellow M&M taste? How does it differ from the way a green M&M tastes?

Finally, ask everyone to pick out any color of M&M and bite it in half, holding on to one of the halves. Tell teenagers to look at the inside of the M&M, then to compare it to M&Ms of different colors that others have. Ask:

• What do all of the M&M's candies look like inside?

Say: **No matter how M&M's look on the outside, they're all the same on the inside. That's how God sees us. No matter what we look like on the outside, God cares about what our hearts are like.**

Read aloud 1 Samuel 16:7. Then say: **God is not concerned with whether we're beautiful or well-built, or with our skin color or our eye color or our hair color. He sees inside of us and loves us all the same.**

Making a Good Impression

Theme: Living out faith

Scripture: Colossians 4:2-6

Supplies: You'll need a Bible, paper, several ink pads, and a few rags for cleanup.

In this activity, students will evaluate how their example affects the lives of the people around them.

Distribute paper to each participant and one stamp pad for every three or four teenagers to share. Direct students to use the supplies to place their fingerprints on the blank sheets of paper. See that cleanup rags are available as students complete their sets of prints. After everyone has finished, have group members write on each other's pages the influence each person has had on their lives. Then ask:

• Have any of you ever been fingerprinted before? How is a person identified by their fingerprints?

• Why is fingerprinting a common practice? What purpose does it serve?

Read aloud Colossians 4:2-6, paying special attention to verses 5 and 6.

Say: **Just as our fingers leave an invisible mark on everything we touch, every day we leave an impression on every person we encounter.**

Ask:

- **What kind of impression are you leaving on your friends?**
- **How can the acquaintances you meet daily identify you as a Christian?**

Discuss together different ways Christians can live their faith and touch the lives of those around them.

Manna or Medicine?

Theme: Discipline

Scripture: Romans 8:28; Hebrews 12:7-11; James 1:2-3

Supplies: You'll need a Bible, plastic spoons, water, unsweetened powdered drink mix, and paper cups.

Use this lesson to show how God cares for his children through discipline.

Have group members form pairs, and give each pair two plastic spoons and a paper cup. Pour a small amount of powdered drink mix in each cup, and add water.

Ask group members to pretend that the drink is medicine, and have partners feed each other a spoonful of the substance. Then ask:

- **Why do parents give their kids medicine?**
- **If you were sick and your parents gave you bad-tasting medicine to make you better, would you blame your parents for the bad taste of the medicine or thank them for helping to make you well? Why?**
- **What are some good things that come from bad-tasting medicines?**

Say: **When a loving parent gives medicine to a child, the parent is trying to help the child, not hurt him or her. It's the same with God's discipline.**

Ask several volunteers to read aloud Romans 8:28; Hebrews 12:7-11; and James 1:2-3. Then say: **When we're God's children, he cares for us better than any earthly parents could, no matter how much they love us. And sometimes God needs to discipline us to make us more like himself.**

Ask:

- **How does God discipline us?**
- **What kinds of things does God use to discipline or guide us?**

Say: **When we begin to see God in every aspect of our lives—even the times we need discipline—we can accept every situation in our lives with thankfulness.**

My Cup Runneth Over

Theme: God's love

Scripture: Psalm 23

Supplies: You'll need a Bible, two large cups, water, a small dropper such as an eyedropper, and a large pitcher of water.

Use this demonstration to illustrate the difference between seeking fulfillment through the world and through God.

Say: **We're going to examine one of the most well-known psalms, Psalm 23. It was written by King David. David knew that only God met all of his needs. Let's look at how God meets our needs and how the world meets our needs.**

Put out the two cups. Say: **This first cup represents the person trying to be fulfilled by the world.**

Ask:

- **What different ways do people seek fulfillment in the world?**

As each student names a way people seek the world's fulfillment, have that person use the dropper to squeeze a drop of water into the first cup.

After everyone has had a turn to drop water into the cup, say: **This second cup represents the person seeking through Christ.**

Hold the cup still and fill it with water from the pitcher. Ask a volunteer to read aloud Psalm 23, then repeat verse 5. Ask:

- **How does seeking fulfillment through Christ compare to seeking fulfillment through the world? Why?**
- **Are you seeking fulfillment from God or from the world?**
- **In what areas of your life do you feel unfulfilled?**
- **How can Christ help you fulfill those areas?**

Say: **God wants us to be fulfilled, but that can only happen through him. If we turn to the world for fulfillment, we'll come up empty. But when we turn to God, our lives are like a cup overflowing with God's blessings.**

No Better You

Theme: Self-esteem
Scripture: Genesis 1:26-27
Supplies: You'll need a Bible and modeling clay.

This is a wonderful way to teach youth about individuality and what it means to be created in God's image.

Begin by reading aloud Genesis 1:26-27. Then ask:

• **What do you think this Scripture means when it says human beings are created in the image of God?**

Say: **Each one of us is unique, yet each of us is made in the image of God. Each of us has a design and purpose. Each of us has the ability to show God's love, goodness, and other aspects of his character to others. No one will ever be created who is exactly like us. Each of us has something unique to offer the world and God.**

Distribute the modeling clay. Invite each person to flatten a piece of modeling clay until it's large enough to press his or her hand into. Invite each teenager to make an impression of his or her hand in the clay. Then encourage youth to compare their hand prints. Ask:

• **What are some obvious differences you see in everyone's hand prints? What are some similarities?**

• **Why do you think God designed our hand prints to be so different?**

Say: **When we look at our hand prints and the hand prints of others in our group, it's obvious that no two of us are alike. We are all different. And yet each of us has been created in the image of God. Remember: No one can do a better job of being you than *you*.**

Ask:

• **If you could, what ideas would you like to work on to make the world a better place?**

• **How do you plan to use your God-given abilities and ideas?**

After listening to each person's hopes and dreams, close by collecting the clay casts and displaying these, along with each person's name, in a prominent place in the room.

Only One Right Answer

Theme: Salvation

Scripture: John 14:6

Supplies: You'll need a Bible, a combination padlock for every four students, index cards.

Use this activity to illustrate that the only way to get to God is through Jesus Christ.

Before the activity, make a master list of all the locks and their combinations so you won't get them mixed up. Then, for each lock, write on an index card a set of numbers that correspond to the correct combination but that are mixed up. For example, if a lock's combination is 6-20-37, you might write "70362" on the card.

Have students form groups of four, and distribute a padlock and corresponding index card to each group. Explain that the numbers listed on their cards contain the correct numbers to the locks' combinations but that the numbers are all mixed up. Challenge groups to open the locks using various combinations of the numbers listed.

After several minutes, gather everyone back together. Ask:

• **How difficult or easy was it for your group to open the lock? Why?**

Reveal the correct combinations to each group, and allow them to open their locks if they haven't already. Ask:

• **How many combinations unlocked each of these locks?**

Say: **Once you know the right answer, it's easy to open the lock, isn't it? Many people today are searching for God in all sorts of ways—through doing good works, going to church, practicing different religions, and so on—but their search is in vain because they don't know the One who can get them to God—Jesus Christ. Often these people are frustrated just as you might have been frustrated when trying to open the locks.**

Ask a volunteer to read aloud John 14:6. Ask:

• **What does this verse tell us about the way to God?**

• **How is Jesus like the true lock combinations?**

Say: **Just as there was only one correct lock combination, there is only one correct way to God—through Jesus Christ. He is the combination that opens God to us. What good news to share with others who are searching!**

Out of the Frying Pan

Theme: Refined faith

Scripture: 1 Peter 1:6-7

Supplies: You'll need a Bible, eggs, plates, a wooden spoon, salt and pepper, forks, and an electric skillet.

Use this lesson to help students understand that their faith is purified and strengthened as it is tested through adversity.

Gather teenagers around the electric skillet. Ask a volunteer to fry an egg in the skillet. As the egg cooks, ask the group members to discuss these questions:

• **If that egg were a person, how would that person be feeling right now?**

• **What good can result if we turn this egg at just the right time and take it off when it's cooked just right?**

• **What bad can result if we leave the egg on the heat for too long?**

Ask another volunteer to read aloud 1 Peter 1:6-7. Ask several volunteers to restate the Scripture in their own words. Then ask youth to compare the cooking egg to the Scripture.

Say: **Growing and learning often require us to go through some discomfort. It's not always fun, but we can stand the heat if we keep our eyes on the end result.**

Ask:

• **How can you make it through the heat that refines you?**

• **In what ways have you grown and learned from refining heat?**

During the discussion, be sure to help youth distinguish between tragedies like abuse or car wrecks and refining fire—things God sends to help us grow in endurance, persistence, compassion, joy, and so on.

As people name ways they've been refined, allow them to break an egg into the skillet. Cook the eggs and serve them as a snack to illustrate the good that can come from refining fire.

Picture Frames

Theme: God's love

Scripture: Zephaniah 3:17; 1 John 3:1

Supplies: You'll need a Bible, inexpensive picture frames, poster board, markers, scissors, and magazines.

Use this lesson to help students recall at least one way God has shown them his love.

Give each person a picture frame and a piece of poster board. Have students cut the poster board to fit their frames. Ask:

• **What do the pictures in your home look like?**

Instruct teenagers to re-create some of their specific memories (good or bad) as pictures on the pieces of poster board, either by drawing or by cutting pictures from magazines to symbolize the memories.

After about ten minutes, have students place their pictures in the picture frames. Next have each person find a partner. Ask partners to share with each other their happiest memories. After a few minutes of sharing, gather everyone together again and share what they discussed.

Read aloud Zephaniah 3:17.

Say: **God is with us during our happiest times, and he takes just as much delight in those times as we do. But when we're going through difficult times, we can also be encouraged by the fact that God is with us and will take care of us.**

Ask a volunteer to read aloud 1 John 3:1. Say: **We are God's children, and his joy and love for us as his children are great. Take a moment to imagine that, as children of God, all our pictures are on his mantel.**

Have teenagers close their eyes. Say: **Think of a happy memory that you and**

God share. Thank God for the joy the memory brings and for his amazing love for you as his child.

Give youth a few moments to spend with God.

Be sure to remind students to take their pictures home as reminders of God's presence during happy and sad times.

Pig Jewelry

Theme: Appearance
Scripture: Proverbs 11:22
Supplies: For every four people you'll need a Bible, a stuffed animal, and several pieces of jewelry.

Use this idea to illustrate that outer beauty is worthless without inner beauty.

Have students form groups of four. Give every group a stuffed animal and some jewelry. Say: **Dress up your animal for a beauty contest.**

After a few minutes, let each group display their bejeweled animal, then have them discuss the following questions in their foursomes:

- **What three words would you use to describe these animals? Why?**
- **What would you think of someone who put real jewelry on a real animal?**
- **Read Proverbs 11:22 with your foursome. How is outer beauty without inner beauty or wisdom like a pig wearing jewelry?**
- **Do you think most people pay more attention to their physical appearance or their inner qualities like wisdom and a beautiful spirit? Why is that?**
- **What can you do to make sure your inner qualities are as attractive as your external appearance?**

Say: **There's nothing wrong with having an attractive outward appearance, but let's focus on what really matters: our inner qualities.**

Pillow Talk

Theme: Unity
Scripture: Colossians 3:14
Supplies: You'll need a Bible.

Use this object lesson during a sleepover or lock-in to remind teenagers about the importance of unity and love in the body of Christ.

Have all the teenagers bring a pillow to the meeting. Gather everyone together, and have students lie down with their pillows to discuss these questions:

- **How long have you had your pillow?**
- **What is your pillow made of?**
- **What makes your pillow so comfortable to you?**

Say: **No matter how long we've had our pillows, what our pillows are made of, or how comfortable they have become, one thing is true: All pillows require a covering to keep them together. In fact, a pillow wouldn't be much of a pillow if it were not inside the case.**

Ask students to sit up again. Have a volunteer read aloud Colossians 3:14. Ask:

- **How are the results of being bound together in love like the results of your pillow stuffing being bound together in a case?**
- **How does the way your pillow feels remind you of the way it feels to belong to the body of Christ?**
- **What kinds of things threaten the unity and love that binds Christians together?**
- **How can we practice binding ourselves with other Christians in love and unity?**

Say: **Let's start today by closing in prayer together.** Have the group form a circle and hold hands. Encourage students to pray aloud for unity in the group.

A Place to Rest

Theme: Church
Scripture: Psalm 84:1-4
Supplies: You'll need a Bible, a large pile of extremely soft blankets and silky sheets, pillows, candles, matches or lighter, and cool refreshments.

Use this idea when your group is tired—after a strenuous game of basketball or after your group has worked hard on a fund-raiser, for example. Have volunteers prepare the supplies ahead of time so everything is ready for your tired group. Have the volunteers construct a pile of comforters, silky sheets, and pillows into a big circular human nest. Also ask volunteers to set up a refreshment table and to light the room softly with candlelight.

After the youth have played their game or finished cleaning up after a fund-raiser, tell them you want them to get together as a group and come with you to a special place. Have the youth follow you into the prepared room.

Say: **Get yourself something to drink and eat. When you're finished eating, find yourself a comfortable spot in the human nest that has been prepared for you.**

When everyone is resting in the human nest, read aloud Psalm 84:1-4. Then have the group discuss these questions:

- **We know that God dwells everywhere. However, church is where we come specially to meet and worship God as a family with other Christians. Why does the soul need a place to rest?**
- **Does God like for us to rest? Explain.**
- **This Scripture talks about finding rest and taking time to dwell in God's house. Do you find rest when you come to church? Explain.**
- **We all go through a lot of trials during the week. Our souls get exhausted just as our bodies are exhausted right now. We face temptations and persecutions. Does your soul get enough chances to rest? Explain.**
- **In what ways could you rest your soul?**

Challenge the group to make church attendance a priority for their souls. Remind them that attending church gives us a chance to rest in God's nest. It's a chance to revitalize the soul.

Planting the Seed

Theme: Sharing faith
Scripture: Isaiah 55:10-11
Supplies: You'll need a Bible, plant or flower seeds, soil, planters, and a watering can full of water.

Use this demonstration to illustrate how sharing our faith others is like planting a seed God will cause to grow.

Distribute the seeds, and ask:

• Tell of a past experience you had with planting a flower or plant.

• How long did it take the plant to grow?

Say: **Today we're going to plant flowers and plants.**

Distribute the planters or take the group outside to a prearranged planting area on the church grounds. Help students plant the seeds and water them. Afterward, ask:

• How long do you think it will take for each seed to grow?

• What do we need to do to help the seeds grow?

Say: **Planting these seeds is like sharing the Word of God. Sometimes when we share about God, it seems like nothing happens. But God says that if we share his Word, the results will not be empty.**

Ask a volunteer to read aloud Isaiah 55:10-11. Then ask:

• How many of you have told others about faith in God, then nothing seemed to happen? Explain.

• According to Isaiah 55:10-11, what does God promise?

• How should we respond to this promise?

• What can we do to continue nurturing the seed we've planted after we share our faith with someone?

Close by asking students to pray for people they will share their faith with or people with whom they have shared their faith. Be sure somebody waters and cares for the seeds youth have planted. When the plants grow, review the lesson with the group again.

Theme: Holy Spirit

Scripture: Acts 1:8

Supplies: You'll need a Bible and several household appliances, such as a blow dryer, a toaster, or others that run on electricity.

Use this idea to illustrate that Christians need to depend on the power of the Holy Spirit to serve God.

Have youth form as many groups as you have appliances. Set up the appliances, and have each group gather around one appliance. Have groups spend a few minutes using the appliances, then explaining to the other groups how the appliances work. After a minute or so, get everyone's attention. Ask:

- **What is the one thing that all these appliances need to work correctly?**
- **What happens when these appliances don't have their power source?**

Say: **Just as these appliances need electricity to function, we need our power source to serve God. God has given us the Holy Spirit to guide us and to help us do all the things God wants us to do. When we try to function without the power of the Holy Spirit, we quickly become tired and burned out. But when we depend on and use the power of the Holy Spirit, we function the way God intended.**

Ask:

- **Can you think of a time when you depended on the Holy Spirit's power? What happened?**
- **How can you remember to depend on the Holy Spirit's power more?**
- **What helps you to stay plugged in to God's power?**

Say: **Let's thank God for providing us with power through the Holy Spirit and ask God to help us depend more upon that power.** Ask a volunteer to close the lesson in prayer, or offer a prayer for the group yourself.

The Positive Force

Theme: Peace
Scripture: John 14:27
Supplies: You'll need a Bible, and an AA or AAA battery for each student.

Use this lesson to help students understand they can and should always be a positive force for peace in our influence on others.

Have group members form a circle. Give each student a battery, and say: **Just as this battery has a negative force on one end and a positive force on the other, there are both negative and positive forces in the world.**

First have the students hold their batteries with the negative side up and spend some time talking about the negative forces they've seen in the world or in their lives. Encourage everyone to talk about times people have been negative forces on them as well as times they've been negative forces on others.

Then have students hold their batteries with the positive side up and spend time talking about the positive forces they've seen in the world or in their lives. Encourage everyone to talk about times people have been positive forces on them as well as times they've been positive forces on others.

Read aloud John 14:27. Have students discuss times Christ has been a positive force in the midst of a negative event.

Extension Idea

You may also want to hold up a flashlight bulb and have everyone hold their batteries together to light the bulb. Talk about how unity in the church is related to sharing Christ's peace.

Then say: **We all have the potential to be either a negative force or a positive force. It is Christ's peace, a peace that alleviates fear and loneliness, that can help us to be a positive force, no matter what's going on around us. And Christ gives us his peace so we can share that peace with others. Look at your battery. Think of the plus sign as a cross, and think about how you can share Christ's peace with others.**

The Potter and the Clay

Theme: Submitting to God
Scripture: Isaiah 64:8
Supplies: You'll need a Bible and clay.

Use this activity to illustrate the need to submit to Christ rather than depend on ourselves.

Explain to the group that they are going to practice being artists. Give each person a small chunk of clay, and give students time to make a small pot, cup, or anything else they want to make. Most likely, students will not make beautiful masterpieces because most will not have the necessary experience. Ask:

• **How would you rate your own creation on a scale from one to ten, with**

one being "not worth the clay it's using" and ten being a "masterpiece"? Why?

- **How is your creation different from what you'd originally pictured or planned?**
- **How does your creation reflect what happens when people try to take control of their own lives instead of depending on God?**

Say: **When we try to take full control of our own lives, we often make a mess of things. What happens is not what we envision.**

Have a volunteer read aloud Isaiah 64:8.

Say: **Imagine the shape you wanted your clay to take. Since we're not sculptors, we can't even imagine the things this clay can do. God is the sculptor of our lives, and he can shape the clay of our lives into something amazing! But the only way God can begin to sculpt us is if we quit trying to do the work ourselves.**

Ask:

- **How are you allowing God to use you?**
- **Are there parts of your life that you're still trying to sculpt yourself without God? Explain.**
- **How can you begin to give God the control over those areas of your life?**

Have students close by praying to be moldable clay in God's hands.

The Potter's Wheel

Theme: Submitting to God

Scripture: Romans 9:21

Supplies: You'll need a Bible, a potter's wheel, clay, water, and towels for cleanup.

Use this activity to illustrate how God made us for a purpose, and how he's in charge of our lives.

Set up the potter's wheel, and begin forming a simple shape, such as a bowl, with the clay. Then give each person a turn to help shape the bowl. (If you have a small group, let group members each make a bowl.) After the bowl is formed, gather group members in a circle. Ask:

• If you were the potter, how would you decide what to make on your potter's wheel?

• Who was in charge in this activity—you or the clay?

• Could the clay become a beautiful bowl without the potter's help? Explain.

• How is God like a potter?

• How are we like the clay?

Read aloud Romans 9:21.

Say: **God made each of us for a purpose, and he's continually shaping us into the form he wants us to take. Our goal should be to be like the potter's clay—willing to be formed by the potter's hands. Just as the clay on our potter's wheel can't make itself into anything beautiful without the potter's help and knowledge, we can't become what God wants us to be unless we submit to letting our lives be shaped by him.**

Potential Power

Theme: Love

Scripture: Hebrews 10:24-25

Supplies: You'll need a Bible and facial tissues.

Use this lesson to show students some practical ways to show God's love to others and build them up.

Give each teenager a facial tissue, and direct students to make anything they want out of the tissues. For example, a person might create a flower, a tent, or simply shredded bits of tissue. After a few minutes, ask:

• We each had the same materials to start with. Why did we end up in such different places?

• How did you decide what to make?

• Did any of you imitate each other or advise someone what to do with the tissue?

Say: **People are similar to facial tissues. We're all very fragile yet very strong in potential. And we all have the power to affect how others view**

themselves. We can help bring out their potential, or help destroy them.

Have a volunteer read aloud Hebrews 10:24-25. Ask:

- **What is the relationship between how others treat you and how you feel about yourself?**
- **What is the relationship between how you treat yourself and how others treat you?**
- **What words can you use to encourage another person to see and believe the good in herself or himself?**
- **What actions can you use to bring out confidence in someone else?**
- **How can you believe the good in yourself even when others aren't spurring you on?**

Say: **As God's love flows through us, we'll pass it on to others. And love always builds others up, rather than destroying them.**

Extension Idea

Have students make tiny tissue paper flowers as reminders to bring out the good in each other rather than to trash the good of one another.

Prize Possession

Theme: Perseverance
Scripture: Philippians 3:12-14
Supplies: You'll need a Bible, and a small trophy, medal, award plaque, or certificate for everyone in the group.

This lesson will teach the virtues of persistence in the faith and not giving up when difficult times come along.

If you can arrange this before the meeting, invite each teenager to bring in some award or accomplishment that he or she is proud to have earned. Open by allowing each teenager to tell about his or her award or accomplishment. Be sure to affirm everyone in the group.

Say: **Each of us has accomplished something in life. Whether we're a great friend, part of a championship sports team, or a student earning a diploma, we can all be proud of something. Trophies and awards merely help us to remember these important accomplishments. Now let's hear about another type of prize that we're all trying to obtain.**

Read aloud Philippians 3:12-14. Ask:

• **What prize is Paul talking about in this passage?**

• **What is the goal we are all trying to obtain?**

• **What are some of the difficulties that can get in our way?**

• **How can we help each other reach that goal?**

Have the youth form a circle. Distribute an affirmation trophy, award, or certificate to each person.

Say: **Each of you is important in God's eyes. We are all striving toward the prize. This is called perseverance. We have to keep going, just like a runner who must run a race, if we are to reach the finish line. But we are not running alone. God is with us. And so are other people. I'd like for each of you to take this award as a small reminder that you are a spiritual athlete. Don't give up when you encounter difficulties and defeats. Keep on trying. Ask for God's help. And know that God has already planned for our final victory.**

Reflecting the Word

Theme: God's Word

Scripture: James 1:22-25

Supplies: You'll need a Bible, a small mirror for every three students, paper, and pens.

Use this lesson to emphasize the importance of following God's Word in our daily lives.

Have students form groups of three. Give a mirror to each group. Have each person take a turn looking in a mirror and describing what he or she sees. Have one person in each group write down the way the other group members describe themselves.

After several minutes, collect the mirrors. Have the students try to repeat back verbatim the descriptions they gave of themselves. Again, a member of each group should note how others describe themselves.

When everyone has finished, have groups discuss these questions:

• **Was it difficult to remember what you said as you looked in the mirror? Explain.**

• What were the differences in the first and second descriptions people gave?

Have a volunteer read aloud James 1:22-25. Then ask:

• How was this activity similar to looking in the Bible for direction but not doing what it says?

• Why is it so easy to forget what we read in the Word? to forget God's love for us in that Word? to forget who God is in our lives according to that Word?

• How can we remember God's Word? to follow God's Word? to encourage one another to live out this Word?

Say: **It's important to read the Bible. But it's even more important to follow God's Word in our daily lives.**

Renewing Strength

Theme: God's strength
Scripture: Isaiah 40:28-31
Supplies: You'll need a Bible and enough canned goods for each person to have two cans.

Use this idea to help teenagers know that when they "hope in the Lord," he will give them strength.

Give each person two cans, and have them hold the cans with their arms straight out from their bodies. If you don't have cans, just have students hold their arms out. Challenge students to hold their arms this way for one minute. At the end of a minute, note how many students still have their arms out. Ask:

• Was that easier or more difficult than you thought it would be? Why?

• What would make the task easier—aside from setting the cans down?

Read aloud Isaiah 40:28-31, and ask:

• What does it mean to "hope in the Lord"?

• When we hope in the Lord, what will happen? Why?

• How does this apply to us when issues or circumstances weigh us down or overwhelm us?

Have students form pairs, and have one partner hold his or her arms out again, holding the cans. This time, ask the other partner to help by holding up his or her partner's arms under the biceps.

Say: **Our burdens may be pretty heavy sometimes. But if we place our hope and trust in the Lord, he can help us carry our burdens. The Lord might not remove our burdens from us completely, but he will "renew our strength" and make it easier for us to carry them.**

Rock-Solid Foundation

Theme: God's Word

Scripture: Matthew 7:24-27

Supplies: You'll need Bibles; paper; and small building blocks—sugar cubes work well, but don't use Legos, Tinkertoys, or anything else that hooks together.

Use this idea to illustrate the difference between those who put Scripture into practice and those who don't.

Have students form groups of four. Give each group a supply of building blocks. Give half the groups sheets of paper (one per group) and the other half Bibles. Instruct the groups to build the best structure they can in three minutes, using the sheets of paper or the Bibles as the bases on which to build.

After three minutes, let each group display its structure. Ask:

• **What features do you like about each structure?**

• **Which structure would you award as most creative? tallest? most pleasing to the eye?**

Then say: **I'd like to use one final criterion to judge each structure: stability.**

Have each group lift up its structure by picking up the Bible or paper on which the structure is built. The paper-based structures will probably fall down; if they don't, have the groups carry their structures to a designated spot. Moving them should make them topple.

Have a volunteer read aloud Matthew 7:24-27, then ask students to discuss these questions in their groups:

• What are some of the "storms" that you face in your life? Be as specific as possible.

• Have you ever felt as if your life might come crashing down around you? Share a little about that situation. How did you make it through that storm?

• How could relying on and putting into practice Jesus' words help you weather the storms you face? Be specific. Have you ever experienced that stability?

• How did you feel when (or would you have felt if) the structure you made fell apart? How do you suppose Jesus feels when the lives of people he created fall apart because they don't have a stable foundation?

• How did you feel when (or would you have felt if) the structure you made held together? How do you suppose Jesus feels when you stand firm by putting his words into practice?

Have students pray in their groups about storms they are facing or ways they need to put Jesus' words into practice in their lives.

Roots of Faith

Theme: Spiritual growth
Scripture: John 15:1-2; 2 Peter 3:18
Supplies: You'll need a Bible, rulers or tape measures, paper and pens, and a small plant for each person.

Use this activity to encourage group members to put their trust in God as they grow in faith.

First give each person a small plant. Distribute the rulers, paper, and pens. Encourage group members to work in pairs or trios to share supplies and build relationships. Have everyone measure how tall his or her plant is, then record the results.

Then have group members encourage their plants to grow. They can talk to their plants, sing to them, or exhort them to grow. After a minute or so, have students again measure their plants and record the results. Then ask:

• Were your plants any taller the second time you measured them? Why or why not?

• **Do you think plants have to *try* to grow? Explain.**

• **What do plants need to grow successfully?**

• **Where do those elements come from?**

Say: **A plant doesn't have to put forth any effort in order to grow. It doesn't strain or stretch itself to grow. It just lets itself be nurtured by the elements God provides, and consequently grows into the plant God meant it to be.**

Ask a volunteer to read aloud John 15:1-2; 2 Peter 3:18. Ask:

• **How is Christian growth like and unlike the growth of a plant?**

• **What do people need to grow as Christians?**

• **How should we respond in those times when we fear we may not be growing spiritually?**

Say: **It's true that we're not plants which grow with no effort. But it's also true that to grow as Christians, it's not about growing ourselves, but about abandoning ourselves to God's care and nurturing to "grow" us. God knows what he wants us to become, and he knows what we need to get there. If we concentrate all our efforts in staying close to God, he'll take care of "growing" us. He'll "cultivate our soil" and will send both "sun" and "rain" to help us grow. We just have to allow and invite God to work in our lives in order to grow as Christians.**

Rule-Book Review

Theme: God's Word

Scripture: 2 Timothy 3:16

Supplies: You'll need a Bible and a game with which your group members are not familiar. The game can be as simple as an unfamiliar card game; be sure you have written rules to accompany the game.

Use this idea to encourage group members to consult the Bible for guidance in daily living.

Begin by having group members play together whatever game you've chosen. Don't tell them the rules or allow them to read the rules beforehand. After a few minutes, encourage everyone to stop and start over, this time consulting the rules before and during play. After the game, ask:

• **How did you know how to play this game?**

• How did the game go before you read the rules?

• What did you do when you were unsure about a step in playing this game?

• At any time during this game, did you just wait to "feel" what the rules were? Why or why not? What was the result if you did?

• How was consulting the rules of this game like consulting the Bible in our lives?

Read 2 Timothy 3:16.

Say: **When we don't know how to play a game, it's natural to consult the rule book. But in life, people often make decisions based on feelings and emotions rather than on the rule book given by God—the Bible. God knew the questions we'd face, and he gave us the answers in the Bible. Going through life without looking at the Bible is about as effective as trying to play an unfamiliar game without looking at the rules.**

Seeing God's Hand

Theme: Creation
Scripture: Psalm 19:1-11
Supplies: You'll need Bibles.

This idea is especially appropriate in nature settings—retreats or camping trips, for example—to open students' eyes to a revelation of God through viewing what he has created.

Have students open their Bibles to Psalm 19:1-11. Have several volunteers take turns reading the verses. Afterward, ask students to point out the two ways the chapter says that God reveals himself (through nature in verses 1-6 and through Scripture in verses 7-11). Instruct students to take five minutes to find either:

• something from nature that shows God's handiwork and that you find to be particularly impressive, or

• a favorite Bible verse or passage, or a verse that speaks of his craftsmanship in creating us.

After five minutes, have the group gather together again. Have students form groups of four and take turns sharing with their group members what they found.

Have teenagers who found something in nature talk about:

• why they chose the item,

• what the item reveals to them about God, and

• how the item makes them feel or think about God when they see it.

Have teenagers who chose a favorite verse or passage read it and talk about:

• why they chose the Scripture,

• what the Scripture reveals to them about God, and

• how the Scripture makes them feel or think about God.

When everyone has shared, have the whole group stand in a circle and hold hands for an "open eyes" prayer. Here's how it works: Everybody finds something for which to praise or thank God. Go around the circle and let everyone pray a sentence out loud with eyes open.

A Sense of God

Theme: Faith

Scripture: Matthew 13:16-17

Supplies: You'll need a Bible, binoculars, and a magnifying glass.

Use this activity to explore assurance of God's existence in times of doubt.

For this activity, you might take your group outside on a sunny day.

Have the students sit in a circle, facing outward. Then ask:

• How do you know God exists?

Pass the binoculars around the circle. Have each student take a look through the binoculars and tell the rest of the class the first thing they see.

As each student identifies something through the binoculars, ask that student:

• How is what you see proof of God's existence?

• How might someone who doesn't believe in God see this item differently?

When everyone has finished, begin passing around the magnifying glass, allowing each student to identify something close-up. Ask the students the same questions.

Repeat the activity again, this time asking each student to close his or her eyes and listen for something that's proof of God's presence.

Ask a volunteer to read aloud Matthew 13:16-17. Then tell your students that when they feel doubt about the existence of God, they can open their eyes and ears, and ask God to make himself known to them.

Shine Like Stars

Theme: Sharing faith
Scripture: Matthew 5:13-16
Supplies: You'll need a Bible and a flashlight.

This is a great object lesson to use on a clear night, especially during a camp out or a retreat. Use the stars to illustrate how students can radiate the pure love of Jesus Christ at school and in their social circles.

Have everyone lie down on their backs with their eyes facing the sky. Say: **Imagine that every person you know is standing in a field. Think of *everyone* you know—your friends, your teachers, your family. Be sure to include the people who you see every day that you may not ever speak to.**

After a few moments, continue: **Now imagine that all those people are strands of light and that light is scattered in the sky above you. There are bright stars and faint stars. There are people who radiate light. Imagine that the light comes from kindness, love, and purity.**

After a few moments, continue: **There are other stars that are faint. They may be losing their brightness. Some create holes of darkness around themselves. Imagine that the holes of darkness are because of complaining, arguing, or gossip.**

After a few moments, continue: **Now think for a moment. Which kind of star are you? Do you radiate light? Do you shine because of your love for God and others? Are you strong and bright, or are you weak and dim? Do you create holes of darkness or beacons of hope for others?**

Using the flashlight to help you see, read aloud Matthew 5:13-16. Then have the group spend some time in silent prayer. Challenge your students to ask God to help them shine brighter or give up the things in life that have dulled their shine.

Extension Idea

Matthew 5:13-16 is a great Scripture to have your teenagers memorize. As they lie under the stars, the students could repeat the Scripture every time they see a shooting star, a satellite, an airplane, or anything else that moves across the sky. Encourage your group to meditate upon the Scripture's words and the meaning each time they repeat the verses.

Skeins of Sin

Theme: Forgiveness
Scripture: Psalm 103:12
Supplies: You'll need a Bible and, for every four students, one skein of black yarn.

Use this activity to illustrate that when we are forgiven, God no longer sees our sin.

Have youth form groups of four. Give each group a skein of yarn, and explain that the groups' goal is to unroll their entire skein of yarn around the meeting facility. They must use the whole skein and cannot go into the same room twice. Tell groups that when they're done, they need to return to the meeting room.

When everyone has returned to the meeting room, ask:

- **How far were you able to go with your skein of yarn?**
- **Were you able to see the beginning of your skein when you got to the end?**

Read aloud Psalm 103:12. Say: **When we ask God to forgive us, he removes our sins as far as the east is from the west.**

Ask:

- **How was your experience with the yarn similar to this verse?**
- **How then should we respond when we have sinned?**

Have students roll up their skeins of yarn.

Spam Competition

Theme: Perseverance
Scripture: 1 Corinthians 9:24-25; Hebrews 12:1-3
Supplies: You'll need a Bible, and five cans of Spam.

Have your group do this activity to review the need to persevere in our faith.

Have kids form five groups. Each group should pick a representative for a Spam-eating contest. Have the eaters sit down at a table and compete to be first to eat their Spam. Encourage teams to cheer wildly.

When the contest is over, have a volunteer read aloud 1 Corinthians 9:24-25. Ask:

• **How did you prepare for the Spam-eating competition? How do people prepare for other competitions?**

• **How does that compare to the effort you put into running the spiritual race?**

Ask another volunteer to read aloud Hebrews 12:1-3. Ask:

• **How did the group's cheers affect your Spam-eating performance? How do spectators and other competitors affect people in other kinds of competitions?**

• **What kinds of spiritual spectators and fellow competitors do you have available to help you? How can they help you to persevere spiritually?**

• **What other kinds of things helped you persevere in this Spam-eating competition? What would have helped you do better?**

• **What else do you need in your spiritual life to keep you going?**

Say: **Just as one would never run in a state track meet with ankle weights and a tire hugging their hips, people serious about their faith do their best to follow God. It's not always easy to keep trying; competitors often face setbacks. But we have many resources available—even Jesus himself—to help and encourage us. We can make it!**

Stains of Unforgiveness

Theme: Forgiveness
Scripture: Isaiah 1:18; Matthew 6:14-15
Supplies: You'll need a Bible, eraser board, markers, newspaper, and baby wipes.

Use this idea to illustrate the stain that unforgiveness leaves on our lives. Help participants to understand that failing to forgive others can hurt us more than we think.

Have teenagers form two groups. Give each group some newspapers and markers. Ask group members to brainstorm for reasons that people fail to forgive others. As volunteers share their answers, have them write one on each piece of newspaper.

After several minutes of brainstorming, ask:

• **What's it like when someone hurts you?**

• **Why can it be difficult to forgive someone who's hurt you?**

• **How does it feel to hold a grudge and choose not to forgive someone?**

Explain that each group may form balls with the newspaper. Ask participants to think of people or things that have hurt them in the past as they form each ball.

Give students a few minutes to form their newspaper balls. Then explain that on your count, the two teams will throw their balls at the other side for one minute. Tell youth that each group is to try and get rid of all the newspaper balls on its side.

Have groups begin, and then call time after a minute has passed. Then ask groups to open the balls of newspaper and read aloud some of the items that ended up on their sides.

Ask everyone to sit down to discuss these questions:

• **What was it like to throw the newspaper balls? to get hit by the newspaper balls?**

• **How is what happened to your hands like what happens to us on the inside when we hold grudges and choose not to forgive?**

• **How was throwing the newspaper balls like what we do with anger and frustration when we refuse to forgive?**

Say: **When we refuse to forgive others, there's only one place for unforgiveness to go—around. We will start "throwing our pain around" at others. When we choose not to forgive, we often think we are hurting the other person but are really hurting ourselves and the people around us more.**

Ask a volunteer to read aloud Matthew 6:14-15.

Say: **Just as the newspaper balls stained your hands, our souls can be stained by unforgiveness. We need to learn to forgive those who hurt us because unforgiveness hurts us and hurts our relationships with God.**

Have a volunteer read aloud Isaiah 1:18. Then invite the group to brainstorm for ways that they can be forgiving and restore their relationships with others and with God. As each student shares an idea, write it on the eraser board and hand the student a baby wipe to wash his or her hands.

After a few minutes of brainstorming, ask:

• How do your hands now reflect what happens when we forgive others?

To close, distribute baby wipes to anyone who hasn't yet washed his or her hands. Give students a few minutes to pray silently for forgiving hearts. As they pray, students can clean their hands. Don't forget to collect and recycle the newspaper after the activity is over.

Star Light, Star Bright

Theme: Living out faith
Scripture: Philippians 2:14-16
Supplies: You'll need a Bible, a flashlight, and glow-in-the-dark stars. You'll also want to conduct this object lesson in a room that can become very dark.

Use this activity to illustrate our role as Christians in the world.

Begin by handing a glow-in-the-dark star to each student. Then turn off the lights. Ask:

• What do you like about stars?

• How would the night be different without stars?

Use the flashlight to read aloud Philippians 2:14-16. Ask:

• Why does our society need people to shine like stars with the word of life?

• How can we be like stars in our world?

Pray that each student can be a star in the world. Have teenagers keep their glow-in-the-dark stars as reminders of their role.

Stick to Christ

Theme: Submitting to God
Scripture: Romans 12:2
Supplies: You'll need a Bible, two craft sticks, one balloon, masking tape, pencils, and a safety pin.

Use this activity to introduce the idea that we need to conform to Christ instead of the world.

Give each person two pieces of masking tape and a pencil, and blow up and tie off the balloon. Ask:

- **What are some things that we depend on to keep us healthy?**
- **What specific things do we trust to keep us safe?**
- **What are some things that we think will make us happy?**
- **What are some other ways that we trust in the world?**

Say: **On one piece of masking tape, write down the one thing in the world that you really depend on or trust—a friend or your savings account, for example. Then put your piece of tape on the balloon.**

Ask:

- **For what kinds of things do you trust God?**
- **Why do you trust God?**
- **How has your life, your personality, or your behavior become more like Christ?**
- **What is one area of your life that you really trust Christ to take care of instead of the world?**

Say: **Write down on your other piece of masking tape one thing in your life that you have chosen to give to God. Then place that piece of tape on the cross.** Create a cross using the two craft sticks and pieces of group members' masking tape.

Ask a volunteer to read aloud Romans 12:2.

Say: **When we conform to the world, when we trust the world to take care of us** (pause and stick the safety pin into the balloon)**, we will be disappointed. The world and the things of the world eventually cave in or crumble. However, when we put our trust and hope in Christ** (pause and stick the safety pin into the craft-stick cross)**, the cross is solid. Christ can handle any pressure and always remains the same. So what will you conform your life and mind to—Christ or the world?**

Strive for Purity

Theme: Sexual purity
Scripture: Genesis 2:18-25
Supplies: You'll need a Bible; super glue; and scraps of paper, plastic, or rubber.

This object lesson will demonstrate that sexual intimacy outside of a marriage commitment is sure to cause pain to the parties involved.

Have youth form pairs, and suggest that they spend a minute or so bonding scraps of paper, plastic, or rubber together with super glue. Next lightly suggest that pairs glue their hands together. When they refuse to do so, ask:

• **What makes this a painful or poor idea?**

• **What might be the consequences of gluing your hands together?**

• **How is being glued to another person like the bond established when two people engage in sex?**

• **What are the consequences of breaking that bond?**

Say: **An intimate relationship outside of the protective commitment of marriage results in a painful separation. God's desire for our sexual purity is meant to protect us from pain.**

Read aloud Genesis 2:18-25, emphasizing verse 24.

Say: **Adam and Eve didn't have parents, so it's clear that this passage was intended for us. The union described is a strong bond not meant to be broken.**

Have students try to separate the scraps they glued together. Ask:

• **How is this tube of glue like the physical and emotional intimacy of a sexual relationship?**

• **How do the scraps you pulled apart reflect what happens when we try to break apart the union formed by a sexual relationship?**

• **What does this exercise tell you about why it's important for sexual intimacy to be saved for marriage?**

• **How does a marriage commitment protect people?**

Encourage students to each determine a commitment of faithfulness to God and to their future spouse. Have youth pray to God, telling him about their commitments.

Team Spirit

Theme: Unity
Scripture: 1 Corinthians 12:27
Supplies: You'll need a Bible, paper, markers, and a school mascot or logo.

Use this activity to teach the unity of the church and what it means to work together for a common good.

Display the school mascot or logo, then ask:

• **How would you describe the significance of the school mascot and what it represents?**

• **How does the mascot help students feel a sense of identity or unity?**

Have the youth form smaller groups. Ask a volunteer to read aloud 1 Corinthians 12:27. Distribute paper and markers to each group.

Say: **I'd like for each group to create a mascot or logo for our youth group. This mascot or logo should help us remember what it means to be a part of each other's lives and part of this group we call the church. The logo might also help us to remember that we are all a part of the body of Christ—the church.**

After a few minutes, allow each group to display what it has created and talk about the symbolism of the logo. Affirm each group's efforts. When every group has shared, ask:

• **How might these mascots or logos help us to have a greater team spirit?**

• **Which of these mascots or logos would help us to see the power that comes from being together and working as one people?**

Close by inviting the entire youth group to work at creating a youth group song or something else that might evoke a feeling of cooperation and unity.

TLC

Theme: God's care
Scripture: Psalm 46:1-3
Supplies: You'll need a Bible, markers, and balloons.

Use this activity to help group members recognize, appreciate, and trust God's care for them.

Begin by giving each group member an uninflated balloon. Explain that for this activity, youth are to pretend that the balloons are babies. Tell group members to "breathe life" into their balloon "babies" and to tie off the balloons. Then let students use markers to draw faces and write names on their balloon babies.

Explain that students must feed, rock, and otherwise care for their babies. Encourage group members to care for their babies by using such statements as "Uh oh! I hear crying. Better rock those babies" and "Time for the 2 a.m. feeding!" If you'd like, you could carry this activity through your entire meeting time, breaking into your lesson at intervals to remind students to care for their babies. Then ask:

- **What was it like to take care of your "baby"?**
- **Why do people spend so much time taking care of babies?**
- **What do babies do to earn such good care?**
- **How is taking care of a baby like how God takes care of us?**

Say: **Now let's pretend that these "babies" have grown up a few years and are just about to start kindergarten.**

Ask:

- **If you were this child's parent, would you still feed, clothe, and care for the child? Why or why not?**
- **What are some ways God continues to care for us?**

Read aloud Psalm 46:1-3. Say: **God is our perfect Father. He knows what we need before we do, and he provides for all of our needs because he loves us.**

Trading Gum

Theme: Peer pressure
Scripture: Matthew 10:22
Supplies: You'll need a Bible; two or three different kinds of gum—enough for each student to have one piece of each kind of gum—and a bowl.

Use this lesson to helps students experience how strong peer pressure can sometimes be.

Place the gum in a bowl, and tell students how many pieces of gum they may take. Ask youth not to chew the gum yet. Explain that students will have two minutes to trade gum with others; to do so, they must try to convince others that the flavor of gum they're holding is the best.

After a couple of minutes, call the group together. Tell the youth that they can chew their gum. Ask:

- **Was it difficult to convince your friends that your flavor of gum was the best? Why?**
- **Did any of you feel tempted to switch? Did you switch? Why or why not?**
- **How many switches did you make because you wanted to make someone else happy?**

Ask a volunteer to read aloud Matthew 10:22. Ask:

- **How was this activity like trying to face peer pressure?**
- **What does this Scripture tell you about facing peer pressure?**
- **What are some benefits of standing firm?**

Say: **Peer pressure provides us with temptations that can be difficult to endure. But with God's help, we can say no to temptation.**

True Love

Theme: Love
Scripture: 1 Corinthians 13
Supplies: You'll need Bibles, popular teen magazines, and dating advertisements from a local newspaper.

Use this idea to teach the qualities of true love in a way that hits home with teenagers.

Distribute the magazines and newspaper ads, and invite students to look through them for statements or articles about love. They should select anything that stands out to them whether it's bizarre, moving, or just plain entertaining. After a few minutes, ask volunteers to read the statements aloud. Ask:

- **How do you think some of the people in these stories or advertisements view love?**
- **What do you think these people are looking for in a relationship?**
- **What qualities or words could we use to describe the nature of the love that these people are talking about?**

Say: **The Bible teaches us that there is a more excellent way to understand life and relationships. Let's hear about this more excellent way.**

Have four or five teenagers read aloud different sections of 1 Corinthians 13. Then ask:

- **What words did the Apostle Paul use to describe the true nature of love?**
- **How is it possible to love like this in our interaction with others?**
- **How can these same qualities be used in a dating relationship?**
- **What would it mean to love another person as described in 1 Corinthians 13? What would this love look like in real life?**

Follow up these questions with some frank discussion about dating relationships and some of the pressures teenagers face today when learning how to love others of the opposite sex.

True Refreshment

Theme: Living out faith
Scripture: Revelation 3:15-16
Supplies: You'll need a Bible, a lukewarm can of soda for each person, ice, and cups.

Use this idea to illustrate God's displeasure with us when we allow our faith to become stagnant.

Before the activity, set out the soda cans on a table. Keep the ice and cups hidden until you need them.

Allow everyone to choose a can of soda from the table. After they've had a chance to react to the taste, gather the group together, and ask:

• What would make these drinks better? What's wrong with them now?

• What makes a drink refreshing?

Read aloud Revelation 3:15-16. Ask:

• How is the way the soda tasted similar to the way we present ourselves to God when we allow ourselves to become lukewarm in our faith?

Reveal the cups and ice, and allow everyone to pour their remaining soda into the cups and add ice to their drinks. As they're drinking, ask:

• Why is the soda more appealing now?

• Why does the ice make so much difference?

• How is this similar to the difference following God makes in our lives?

• What do you think makes a person's life "refreshing" to God, as the ice does for this soda?

• How can we keep ourselves refreshing before God?

Say: **If we begin to just go through the motions as Christians, we become ineffective for Christ and displeasing. But when we keep our relationship with God alive, and we obey God, we are refreshing to him and others around us.**

Try Doing It Together

Theme: Unity

Scripture: 1 Corinthians 12:12-13

Supplies: You'll need a Bible and an easy puzzle with the pieces separated into three or four plastic bags.

This activity will show the group that they accomplish more when they work together instead of separately.

Have teenagers form three or four groups. Give each group a bag of puzzle pieces. Ask each group to put its puzzle together.

As the groups realize that they're missing pieces, ask:

• What is difficult about this task?

• What would make this task easier?

Read aloud 1 Corinthians 12:12-13. Ask:

• **How was trying to put together a puzzle without all the pieces like trying to accomplish things in the church without everyone's participation?**

Say: **In order to complete a puzzle, you need all the pieces. Then all the pieces need to fit together a certain way. A youth group is the same way. Everyone has a specific function, and the group can't be whole without each person doing his or her part.**

Ask the groups to gather together. Tell teenagers to combine their puzzle pieces and put the puzzle together. When they're finished, ask:

• **What made the task easier this time?**

• **How does this relate to the Scripture we read? to our group?**

Say: **Isn't it easier to work together as a group rather than to be divided and try to accomplish a task on our own?**

Turn Down the Volume

Theme: Prayer

Scripture: 1 Kings 19:12

Supplies: You'll need a TV, a stereo, a megaphone, a Bible, and a volunteer who's a good reader.

Use this idea to illustrate the need for people to seek God's voice despite distractions.

Set up all the supplies and turn on the TV and stereo. Ask your volunteer to quietly read aloud from the book of Proverbs. Say: **Today we are going to think about listening for God.**

Ask:

• **What makes it difficult to hear God?**

• **In what ways do you try to discover what God is saying to you?**

Explain that the supplies you've set up can be a picture of our world. Turn up the volume on the stereo and TV. Ask a couple of people to talk, and have one volunteer talk on the megaphone. Then point to the Bible.

In a loud voice, say: **Sometimes when we read the Bible, it's hard to hear God speaking because we're listening to so many other things.**

Point to your volunteer. Say: **Sometimes we pray for God to tell us things**

like what he wants us to do after high school or what to say to a friend. [Name of volunteer] **can represent God speaking.**

Ask if students can hear the volunteer. When they say "no," turn off all the other equipment.

Say: **God could use a megaphone to talk to us. But often God speaks through the Bible, or quietly in our hearts. It's often difficult to hear God with so many other "voices" around us.**

Read 1 Kings 19:12.

To close, have teenagers think about ways they can tune out the messages of the world and listen to God's voice more clearly.

Turn Up the Radio

Theme: Sharing faith

Scripture: 1 Corinthians 9:19-23

Supplies: You'll need a Bible, a radio that can pick up a lot of stations, paper, and a pen.

This object lesson works well while traveling in a church van or bus, but you can do it anywhere you have a working radio.

This activity teaches students to see the potentially creative side to sharing their faith. They'll learn that sharing Jesus with different kinds of people sometimes requires creative energy.

Say: **Let's see what's on all the radio stations.**

Have one of the teenagers write down what kind of programming is on each station. Then go through the list and discuss the target audience of each station. Have the volunteer write down the students' conclusions.

Have another volunteer read aloud 1 Corinthians 9:19-23. Say: **Paul shared the love of Jesus with fervor. He shared the good news about Jesus with all kinds of people from all kinds of cultures.**

Ask:

- **What was Paul's message for us when he said, "I have become all things to all men" in the passage we just heard?**

Say: **Paul indicated that we should spread the love of Jesus with everyone from every background. But we must be flexible in doing this because**

people have different perspectives, cultures, and experiences. As a result, we sometimes must be creative when we share our faith.

Next have teenagers form groups of two or three. Give each group a radio station's target audience to look at. Have groups brainstorm for ways they might reach those groups in creative ways given the target audiences' specific needs and backgrounds. After a few minutes, have each group report its ideas.

Then discuss this question:

• **What were some similarities in ways we would share Jesus and his love with each of the target audiences we identified? What were some differences? Why?**

Say: **Understanding people's interests and frame of reference will help us find creative ways to meet their needs and introduce them to Jesus. Be on the lookout for creative light that will show Christ to a dark world.**

Close with a prayer for the Lord to help your group discover how to share their faith with different kinds of people.

Two Masters

Theme: Submitting to God
Scripture: Matthew 6:24
Supplies: You'll need a Bible, and one six-foot length of rope for every three people in your group.

Use this activity to illustrate how difficult it is to serve two masters.

Have youth form groups of three students. Have each trio designate one person to be the "horse" and the other students to be the drivers. Loop a piece of rope around each "horse," and let one driver hold the left rein and the other driver hold the right rein. Have the drivers try to drive their "horses" around for a few minutes (this will work best if the "horses" hold the ropes at waist level).

Then ask:

• Was this activity easy or difficult? Why?

• In this exercise, each "horse" had two drivers. How is this different from the way horses are typically driven or ridden?

• Drivers, did you feel like you were guiding your "horse," or was your other driver setting the direction? Why?

• "Horses," did you feel any confusion during this activity? If so, where did it come from?

Ask a volunteer to read aloud Matthew 6:24. Say: **Jesus said that you cannot serve two masters.**

Ask:

• Can you name some of the masters people try to serve?

• Who or what should be our master? Why?

To contrast serving two masters with serving one master, let the "horses" team up with one driver and discuss how to use the rope to give and receive directions. If you have time, allow students to switch roles.

Voices

Theme: Relationship with Christ

Scripture: John 10:4

Supplies: You'll need a Bible; a cassette player; and a cassette tape with recordings of various voices your group members will recognize—group leaders, pastors, other familiar church members, musical artists, politicians, or sports figures, for example.

Use this activity to illustrate how we can follow Jesus when we know his voice.

Gather everyone in a circle around the cassette player. Explain that you're going to play a tape with a variety of voices on it and that group members are to try to guess who the voices belong to.

After each voice, pause the tape, and ask:

• Who is this? How do you know?

• Do you really trust this person and value his or her opinion? Why?

After you've played all of the voices on the tape, read aloud John 10:4. Say: **You recognized the voices on the tape because you've spent time with those people or you're familiar with them. In the same way, the more you get to know and trust Jesus, the more you'll be willing to follow him. And following Jesus is the best thing you can do.**

Watch Your Tongue

Theme: Speech
Scripture: Proverbs 15:4
Supplies: You'll need a Bible, a fragrant potted herb such as basil or mint, a pungent herb or spice such as dried chili flakes, and a mortar and pestle.

Use this lesson to emphasize to students the importance of using our words to heal and not to crush others.

Gather students around the fragrant plant and pungent spice. Pass around the plant so everyone has a chance to smell it. You may even encourage students to pinch off leaves and crush them, which will increase the aroma.

Then place a bit of the pungent herb or spice into the mortar. Invite each student to take a turn crushing the herb with the pestle and to smell the herb.

After every student has had a chance to experience both smells, have a volunteer read aloud Proverbs 15:4. Then ask:

• How are kind and honest words like the pleasant aroma of the first plant?

• How is the job of the first plant similar to a "tongue that brings healing"?

• How are unkind or deceitful words like the smell of the second plant?

• How is the way we crushed the second plant similar to the way unkind or deceitful words crush the spirit?

• What kinds of words do you believe are helpful to people and build them up?

• What kinds of words and sentiments do you believe are not helpful and will tear people down?

Close by having students pray, asking for God's help in using their tongues to heal instead of to crush.

Whatever Is Pure

Theme: Thoughts

Scripture: Philippians 4:8-9

Supplies: You'll need a Bible and, for every four people, a container of clear tap water and a container of dirty water.

This object lesson can help illustrate the importance of what people allow themselves to think about.

Have the teenagers sit in groups of four. Distribute a container of clear tap water and a container of dirty water to each group. Have groups examine the containers of water and think of as many descriptive words as possible to describe each.

After groups have talked for a couple of minutes, read aloud Philippians 4:8-9. Explain to them that the clear water could represent a pure mind and the dirty water could represent an impure mind. Ask:

- **What would happen if we mixed these two containers of water in one bowl?**
- **How is that like the way impure thoughts affect us?**
- **What kinds of things cause our minds to fill up with thoughts that are not pleasing to God?**

Next say: **Those are some good observations. But now let's spend some time thinking about the clean water.**

Read aloud Philippians 4:8-9 again. Ask:

- **Can you give some examples of true thoughts? noble thoughts? pure thoughts? admirable, excellent, or praiseworthy thoughts?**

Allow students to share as many positive thoughts as possible.

To close, hold up a container of clear water. Say: **When this container is completely full of clear, clean water, there is no room for dirty water. Spending more time thinking about what is lovely, excellent, and praiseworthy would leave little time for gossip, slander, lust, dirty jokes, and anger.**

Challenge teenagers to spend the coming week trying to think as many pure, positive thoughts as possible and to experience the peace that is promised to them in Philippians 4:9.

Who Is God Gonna Use?

Theme: Holiness
Scripture: 2 Timothy 2:20-21
Supplies: You'll need a Bible, a nice-looking drinking glass that's filthy on the inside, disposable plastic or foam cups, and cold sodas.

Use this idea to illustrate that God wants to use people who are clean on the inside.

Before the activity, talk with a student about your plan to single out him or her. This will prevent any misunderstandings or embarrassment.

Ask students to form a circle. Explain that you want to honor someone in the group, then name the participant who you talked to before the activity. Affirm this person in front of the large group. Then explain that you want to give that person a soda as a way of saying "thank you" and of honoring him or her for being such a great person.

Say: **Since you are so special, I want you to drink out of a very special glass. It is one of my favorite glasses.**

Hand the participant the glass that's nice on the outside but dirty on the inside. Allow the student to respond to the dirty glass, and ask him or her to share with the large group what's wrong with the beautiful glass. Pass the dirty glass around the circle to let all the group members see the dirt inside the glass. Ask:

- **Why do we prefer to use things that are clean rather than things that are dirty?**

Say: **I happen to have another cup. It doesn't look very nice on the outside, and it's really inexpensive. It's not as beautiful on the outside as my special glass. However, if you still will let me honor you with a soda, you can drink out of this cup.**

Pass a clean disposable cup around the circle for everyone to see. Pour the soda into the cup, and give it to the student to drink. Ask:

- **In what ways are these two cups different?**
- **Why is cleanliness so important?**

Have a volunteer read aloud 2 Timothy 2:20-21. Ask:

• **How were the two cups like the point expressed in this Scripture?**

• **What do you think is more important to God: the way we look on the outside or the condition of our hearts? Explain.**

Say: **God wants to use people who are clean, who have pure hearts on the inside. God can use people with clean hearts for noble purposes.**

Ask:

• **How can you clean up and offer yourself to God?**

• **What do you need to do this week to make sure you are pure in heart and ready to be used by God?**

Distribute cups and sodas. As participants drink, have them each share with a partner one way they can be cleaner vessels for God.

Who's Better Than Who?

Theme: Judging

Scripture: Matthew 7:1-5

Supplies: You'll need a Bible; a large magnifying glass; a small, ugly hat; a large, obnoxious hat; and a mirror.

Use this demonstration to illustrate how we often look at others and ourselves. Ask:

• **How many of you think that judging others is a problem for Christians? Explain.**

• **In what ways do we judge others?**

• **Why do we judge others?**

Have a volunteer read aloud Matthew 7:1-5.

Ask for a self-confident volunteer. Put the large, obnoxious hat on yourself and have the volunteer put on the small hat. Ask:

• **Would you ever wear these hats? Why or why not?**

• **Why are these hats acceptable or not acceptable?**

Ask two more students to wear the hats. Give the magnifying glass to the person wearing the large, obnoxious hat, and encourage him or her to examine the small hat for faults. Then have the student with the large hat look in the mirror.

Have the two volunteers pass the hats to another pair. Have them repeat the same process with the magnifying glass and the mirror. Then have them pass the hats along. Continue this process until everyone has had a chance to wear a hat.

After the students have worn and examined the hats, put the large hat back on yourself and the small hat on a student. Point to the hat on your head, and say: **Imagine that this hat is all that is wrong with me.** Point to the small hat on the volunteer's head, and say: **Imagine that this hat is all that's wrong with** [name of volunteer]**. People often look at others with a magnifying glass to examine their faults but fail to look at their own faults. Instead of being so worried about others, we need to concentrate on ourselves.**

Why Go It Alone?

Theme: Mentoring
Scripture: Ecclesiastes 4:9-12
Supplies: You'll need a Bible, freshly cut twigs, index cards, and pens or pencils.

Use this lesson to show students the benefits of having a spiritual mentor.

Give each youth a small branch with several tiny branches, preferably one with green leaves still attached. Ask:

- **How long do you think these leaves will stay green and healthy?**
- **How long do you think the twig will stay nourished and supple?**
- **What would this branch need to grow?**

Say: **To be really healthy and to grow really well, this little branch needs the support of a larger tree. Also, the tree needs the branches because these leaves feed the tree through photosynthesis.**

Ask:

- **What do adult believers have that can help or build up younger believers?**
- **What do younger believers have that can help or build up adult believers?**
- **How has an adult given you guidance, a foundation, or encouragement in your walk as a Christian?**

Ask a volunteer to read aloud Ecclesiastes 4:9-12. Ask:

Extension Idea

Have students study celery or clumps of grapes instead of branches. Then students can make a snack to drive home the point that we provide spiritual nourishment for one another.

• **What has an adult taught you about life?**

• **What adult has helped you do the right thing for the right reason, and how did he or she do this?**

• **How can you expand your group of mentoring adults—those who believe in you and help you know what to do?**

Give each person an index card and a pen or pencil. Say: **Write on your card the name of at least one adult you can get to know better. Be sure that person is someone who will help guide you in the right ways. Then take your card with you as a reminder to get to know that person.**

The Wild Wind

Theme: Future
Scripture: Ecclesiastes 8:7
Supplies: You'll need a Bible and, for each student, a balloon and a marker.

Use this lesson to illustrate the futility of trying to know the future.

Give every person a balloon and a marker. Instruct teenagers to write their names on their balloons, blow up their balloons, but not to tie them.

Say: **On the count of three, I want everyone to release the balloon and then try to catch it. Ready? One, two, three!**

Watch as the balloons fly all over the room and the youth attempt to catch them. When everyone has found his or her balloon, have students blow up their balloons again and repeat the exercise.

When everyone has found his or her balloon, ask:

• **Why don't the balloons go in the same direction each time?**

• **Why was it difficult to catch your balloon in the air?**

• **How could you compare this activity to trying to know the future?**

• **Is this a bad thing, or is it kind of a good thing that we don't know everything about what our future holds? Explain.**

Read aloud Ecclesiastes 8:7. Ask:

• How can you remember to trust God to guide your future?

Have students take home their balloons as reminders to trust the future to God.

The Yoke I Give You

Theme: Burdens

Scripture: Matthew 11:28-30; John 14:27; Philippians 4:7

Supplies: You'll need Bibles, a sack containing canned goods, and a pillow in a case.

Use this object lesson to contrast the weight of our earthly concerns with the sense of freedom and relief that comes from knowing Jesus.

Have students form a circle. Pick up the heavy sack, and have kids pass it around the circle several times.

As the students start to tire, have them stop. Then have them repeat the activity with the pillow, this time passing it in the opposite direction.

After teenagers have passed the pillow around the circle several times, read aloud Matthew 11:28-30. Ask:

• What are some of the burdens you have carried?

• In what way has Jesus given you rest from your burdens?

• What do you think is Jesus' yoke or burden in this verse?

• Why is his burden light rather than heavy?

Say: **In John 14:27 and again in Philippians 4:7, Jesus promises peace to his followers.**

Have two students read these verses aloud, then ask:

• What correlation do you see between Jesus' promise of peace and Jesus' promise of rest for our souls?

• How can we take Jesus up on his offer?

Encourage students to spend several minutes sharing "burdens," such as prayer requests and needs. As they do, have each person sharing remove a can from the heavy sack until it's empty. Then close in prayer, addressing the concerns students have shared.

You Visited Me

Theme: Reaching out

Scripture: Matthew 25:34-40

Supplies: You'll need a Bible, a box of ready-made generic invitations, a box of blank greeting cards, and pens.

Use this idea to show teenagers the plight of those who are continually being separated from society.

Hand out the invitations. Ask each student to fill in the blanks on the invitation with an idea for a great party. Tell them to make the party realistic—a party that could actually happen. Party ideas include pizza, videos, football, swimming, and so on.

When the group is done creating the cards, collect them.

Say: **I'm going to read all the invitations aloud to you. I want you to pretend that these parties are really going to happen in our community. I want you to pretend that all your friends are going to be there.**

After reading the invitations aloud, ask:

- **How would you feel if you received invitations to all those parties?**
- **How would you feel if you knew those parties were happening, but you weren't invited to any of them?**

Have the students brainstorm about why people are left out of social happenings—being expelled from school, facing personal problems, dealing with an illness, and moving to a new school, for example. Ask:

- **Do you know people who are left out? Why does that happen to them?**
- **Do you know people who have been taken away from their social circles? How do you think they feel?**

Read aloud Matthew 25:34-40. Then have the youth brainstorm reasonable ways that teens can reach out to those who have been separated from fun and activities. Ask the youth to think of ways that they think Christ would have them reach out to others without putting themselves at risk.

Hand out the blank greeting cards. Say: **Think of someone you know who may feel isolated right now. Do you know a student who's been expelled from your school? Do you know someone who's lost his or her job? Do you**

know someone having trouble at home? Do you know someone who lives all alone? Fill in that person's name on your card.

Now write a note to the person you thought of. Let these people know that you're thinking of them.

After students have finished writing, say: **You can choose to send your card to the person you wrote to or not. If you don't think sending a card is appropriate, keep the card as a reminder to reach out to that person and others who are isolated. I challenge you to do something concrete this week to reach out to someone who may have been forgotten.**

Indexes

Scripture Index

Theme Index

Group Publishing, Inc.
Attention: Product Development
P.O. Box 481
Loveland, CO 80539
Fax: (970) 679-4370

Evaluation for
PointMaker™ Object Lessons for Youth Ministry

Please help Group Publishing, Inc. continue to provide innovative and useful resources for ministry. Please take a moment to fill out this evaluation and mail or fax it to us. Thanks!

● ● ●

1. As a whole, this book has been (circle one)

not very helpful — very helpful

1 2 3 4 5 6 7 8 9 10

2. The best things about this book:

3. Ways this book could be improved:

4. Things I will change because of this book:

5. Other books I'd like to see Group publish in the future:

6. Would you be interested in field-testing future Group products and giving us your feedback? If so, please fill in the information below:

Name ______________________________

Church Name ______________________________

Denomination ____________________ Church Size ____________

Church Address ______________________________

City ____________________ State ____________ ZIP ____________

Church Phone ______________________________

E-mail ______________________________

Bible Study Series

Give Your Teenagers a Solid Faith Foundation That Lasts a Lifetime!

Here are the *essentials* of the Christian life—core values teenagers *must* believe to make good decisions now...and build an *unshakable* lifelong faith. Developed by youth workers like you...field-tested with *real* youth groups in *real* churches...here's the meat your kids *must* have to grow spiritually—presented in a fun, involving way!

Each 4-session **Core Belief Bible Study Series** book lets you easily...

- Lead deep, compelling, *relevant* discussions your kids won't want to miss...
- Involve teenagers in exploring life-changing truths...
- Help kids create healthy relationships with each other—and you!

Plus you'll make an *eternal difference* in the lives of your kids as you give them a solid faith foundation that stands firm on God's Word.

Here are the Core Belief Bible Study Series titles already available...

Senior High Studies

Title	ISBN
Why **Authority** Matters	0-7644-0892-5
Why **Being a Christian** Matters	0-7644-0883-6
Why **Creation** Matters	0-7644-0880-1
Why **Forgiveness** Matters	0-7644-0887-9
Why **God** Matters	0-7644-0874-7
Why **God's Justice** Matters	0-7644-0886-0
Why **Jesus Christ** Matters	0-7644-0875-5
Why **Love** Matters	0-7644-0889-5
Why **Our Families** Matter	0-7644-0894-1
Why **Personal Character** Matters	0-7644-0885-2
Why **Prayer** Matters	0-7644-0893-3
Why **Relationships** Matter	0-7644-0896-8
Why **Serving Others** Matters	0-7644-0895-X
Why **Spiritual Growth** Matters	0-7644-0884-4
Why **Suffering** Matters	0-7644-0879-8
Why **the Bible** Matters	0-7644-0882-8
Why **the Church** Matters	0-7644-0890-9
Why **the Holy Spirit** Matters	0-7644-0876-3
Why **the Last Days** Matter	0-7644-0888-7
Why **the Spiritual Realm** Matters	0-7644-0881-X
Why **Worship** Matters	0-7644-0891-7

Junior High/Middle School Studies

Title	ISBN
The Truth About **Authority**	0-7644-0868-2
The Truth About **Being a Christian**	0-7644-0859-3
The Truth About **Creation**	0-7644-0856-9
The Truth About **Developing Character**	0-7644-0861-5
The Truth About **God**	0-7644-0850-X
The Truth About **God's Justice**	0-7644-0862-3
The Truth About **Jesus Christ**	0-7644-0851-8
The Truth About **Love**	0-7644-0865-8
The Truth About **Our Families**	0-7644-0870-4
The Truth About **Prayer**	0-7644-0869-0
The Truth About **Relationships**	0-7644-0872-0
The Truth About **Serving Others**	0-7644-0871-2
The Truth About **Sin and Forgiveness**	0-7644-0863-1
The Truth About **Spiritual Growth**	0-7644-0860-7
The Truth About **Suffering**	0-7644-0855-0
The Truth About **the Bible**	0-7644-0858-5
The Truth About **the Church**	0-7644-0899-2
The Truth About **the Holy Spirit**	0-7644-0852-6
The Truth About **the Last Days**	0-7644-0864-X
The Truth About **the Spiritual Realm**	0-7644-0857-7
The Truth About **Worship**	0-7644-0867-4

Order today from your local Christian bookstore, or write:
Group Publishing, P.O. Box 485, Loveland, CO 80539.